TBR - 8 : 173

D1606060

LOOK OUT!
THE PENTECOSTALS
ARE COMING

LOOK OUT!
THE PENTECOSTALS
ARE COMING

C. Peter Wagner

Creation House
Carol Stream, Illinois

FIRST EDITION

Library of Congress Catalog Card Number 73-77528

ISBN-0-88419-040-4

OTHER BOOKS BY
THE SAME AUTHOR:

THE CONDOR OF THE JUNGLE
  (with Joseph S. McCullough; Fleming H. Revell Co.)
DEFEAT OF THE BIRD GOD
  (Zondervan Publishing House)
LATIN AMERICAN THEOLOGY
  (Eerdmans Publishing Co.)
THE PROTESTANT MOVEMENT IN BOLIVIA
  (William Carey Library)
AN EXTENSION SEMINARY PRIMER
  (with Ralph Covell; William Carey Library)
*A TURNED-ON CHURCH IN AN UPTIGHT
  WORLD* (Zondervan Publishing House)
FRONTIERS IN MISSIONARY STRATEGY
  (Moody Press)
CHURCH/MISSION TENSIONS TODAY
  (editor, Moody Press)

CONTENTS

Look Out! The Pentecostals Are Coming

As Peter Wagner has pointed out in the following pages, Pentecostals see the world-wide advance of the Pentecostal movement as a partial fulfillment, at least, of Joel's prophecy, cited by Peter on the Day of Pentecost, "And it shall come to pass in the last days saith God, that I will pour out my Spirit upon all flesh." (Joel 2:28; Acts 2:17). Not all Pentecostals will agree with Wagner's interpretation of Pentecostal doctrine in every point, but probably all will be satisfied that he emphasizes important factors of church growth to be found in the Pentecostal movement. Wagner a non-Pentecostal himself, nevertheless views the Pentecostal movement with sympathetic understanding, and endeavors to explain their practices in the light of Biblical interpretation and cultural backgrounds. His frankness and openness will be appreciated by Pentecostals, but as he himself points out, the main thrust of the book is to point up the reasons why the Pentecostals have grown, and to encourage non-Pentecostals to learn from their Pentecostal brethren.

Pentecostals themselves give the main credit for church growth in their midst to the moving of the Holy Spirit. They believe that only the Spirit can exalt the Lord Jesus Christ in the way that will bring the multitudes to Him. It would be my hope that non-Pentecostals would seek not only to emulate methods used by Pentecostal people to extend the Kingdom, but that many may sense their need for an increased work of the Spirit in their ministry and churches and open their hearts to the mighty wind of God, which can blow upon dormant churches and cause them to awaken.

Pentecostals themselves have no desire to promote any extra-Biblical emphasis, but do long for the complete fulfillment of what God meant when Joel prophesied "I will pour out my Spirit upon all flesh."

Melvin L. Hodges
Secretary for Latin America and
General Council of the Assemblies of God
West Indies

PREFACE

Much has been written about Pentecostalism in Latin America, but the exciting facts have not yet been gathered together in brief, readable form, combined with a simultaneous attempt to get below the surface and discover just what it is that instead makes Pentecostal churches grow the way they do.

Pentecostal churches in general have been growing at rates significantly higher than almost any other kind of church in Latin America. Scores of people have asked me "Why?" "What are the Pentecostals doing right?" "What are non-Pentecostal churches doing wrong?" These questions are begging to be answered, and many answers are now available.

Fragmentary answers have been given. There is a book on the growth of churches in Argentina where the author analyzes the dynamics of Pentecostal growth there. There is a graduate thesis on Pentecostals in Colombia, and another with a section on the relationship of Pentecostals and Spiritists in Brazil. There is a book written in Spanish by a Pentecostal leader from Chile. There is an article by an Australian who visited Latin America and was astonished at the mushrooming Pentecostal churches. In fact, today the literature is growing so fast that the average person simply cannot keep up with it.

All through this literature one encounters complex and varied growth situations. But we have now come to the point where we can begin to discern certain patterns within the complexity. This is what I am attempting to do here. I do not claim to have read every bit of the literature, but my position allows me to come into contact with a good portion of it. I have spent time in almost every Latin American republic, and a span of sixteen years residing in Latin America. I do feel quite confident that the reasons given here for the growth of Pentecostal churches in Latin America, although perhaps at times overgeneralized, come quite close to the heart of the matter.

The purpose of this book, however, is neither a cold-blooded analysis nor an attempt to be critical. Any movement growing like the Pentecostals is highly vulnerable and could be criticized on many counts. I have chosen not to be critical because of what I consider a higher purpose. I hope that this book will be useful in helping to fulfill the Great Commission in Latin America, and in other parts of the world.

Thus, I hope to speak to many non-Pentecostal churches which have well-defined evangelistic purposes, consecrated personnel, outstanding programs, orthodox doctrinal statements, affluent budgets, exhausting activities, and many years of experience—but which are growing little or not at all. Some years ago, one of these missions, working in Chile in the midst of unseen but burgeoning Pentecostal growth, wrote back home excusing its lack of fruitfulness on the basis that "the Chileans are an almost Islamic population." One can only feel a wave of pity for such a misguided mission. God has something better for it and others like it than failure in the attempt to fulfill the Great Commission to make disciples of all nations.

Prejudice has kept many non-Pentecostals from learning the valuable lessons about effective evangelism in Latin America that Pentecostals can teach. I pray that God will use this book to break down some of those long-standing barriers. My own credential as a non-Pentecostal should help. I have no bill of goods to sell. I am not engaging in promoting my own church or mission or movement. I have simply looked at what God is doing through my Pentecostal brethren, and I can do nothing but praise Him for it.

The harvest in Latin America is great—greater than even the Pentecostals can handle. All laborers are needed in the harvest fields today. No one does well to sit under the shade tree while others toil with sweat and tears to bring in the sheaves. It has not been our intention, but I fear that many of us in Latin America have been doing just that. We should be reaping, but we sharpen our sickles while the harvest rots. We should be fruitful, but we are barren. Sometimes it is because we are in the wrong place at the wrong time.

— 13 —

Sometimes it is because we don't really know how to reap. Our Pentecostal brethren can help us on both counts.

If we only are willing to listen . . .

C. Peter Wagner
Fuller Theological Seminary

Pasadena, California
March, 1973

1

The Phenomenal Growth of

Latin American Pentecostalism

On the morning of January 14, 1909, a Chilean
night watchman had fallen into a deep sleep in
his home in Valparaiso. Suddenly Jesus Christ
appeared to him in a dream, as clearly as if
He had been standing right there in the bedroom.
The sleeping man had been a Christian and a
member of the local Methodist church for some
time, but this had never happened before.

Jesus looked at him and said in a gentle, but
firm, voice, "Wake up. I want to speak to you."

"Yes, Lord!" the startled man replied.

"Go to your pastor and tell him to gather some
of the most spiritual people of the congregation.
They are to pray together every day. I intend
to baptize them with tongues of fire."

Sleep was gone for the day. The man hurried to find his pastor and tell him about the dream— or was it just a dream? For some months, the pastor himself had been anticipating some unusual spiritual blessing. He accepted the dream as a revelation from God. The next afternoon a group of dedicated believers met in the parsonage for prayer. They promised each other that they would continue to pray together at five o'clock each afternoon until the Lord fulfilled His promise.

Extraordinary things began to happen. Believers became deeply concerned for their spiritual lives. Hidden sins were brought to the surface and confessed. Hardened pagans were converted. Several had dreams and visions that confirmed to them that they were on the right road. Great blessing was anticipated and fervently prayed for.

By mid-April the revival had begun. The group in the parsonage in Valparaiso looked upon it as a literal fulfillment of Joel 2:28: ". . . I will pour out My Spirit on all mankind; And your sons and daughters will prophesy, Your old men will dream dreams. . ." The Spirit was falling in great power.

The Pentecostal movement had come to Chile.

The pastor of that Methodist church was Willis C. Hoover, an American missionary, who had been praying that his church in Chile would somehow see the power of the churches in the book of Acts. As far back as 1895, Hoover had attended a church in Chicago which was living in a continuing revival, and he was deeply moved. He longed for something similar in his own life. An earthquake had destroyed their church building, and constructing a new one took much time and energy. It was finished in 1908, giving Hoover more time for spiritual things.

Providentially, a tract from India began a slow transformation in his life. A schoolmate of his wife's, who was working among widowed girls with Pandita Ramabai, had sent it. If the Hoovers had not known the author they might not have read it. But it described in detail how the Holy Spirit had fallen with fire among a group of Christians halfway around the world.

Fascinated, the Hoovers began to correspond with other friends in Venezuela, Norway, and India, who shared with them their experiences with the Holy Spirit. It was at this time that the night watchman had his vision, and the afternoon prayer meeting started.

The struggling church began to grow. Sunday School attendance reached 363 in July, 425 in August, and 527 in September. Worship services were running between 800 and 900 by October.

In spite of the fact that such church growth had not been seen previously in the Chilean Methodist Church, fierce opposition arose against Hoover and the members of his church. The open manifestations of spiritual power were offensive to many. Some local newspaper reporters poked fun at these religious fanatics, and the reports found their way back to the Methodist Missionary Society in New York. One missionary colleague cabled headquarters with the false charge that Hoover had been sentenced by a criminal court in Valparaiso. By the end of 1909 official charges had come against him.

One document accused Hoover of "teaching

the doctrines of raising of hands, the baptism of fire, miracles of faith healing, visions, the gift of tongues, prophecies, predicting the date of Christ's return, falling down under the power of the Holy Spirit, and opposition to organized churches." Such things were said to be "anti-Biblical and anti-Methodist," and before long the Methodist Church had forced Willis Hoover out.

Undaunted, Hoover started separate services in 1910 and founded the Methodist Pentecostal Church. The growth of this church through the years has been phenomenal. Some estimates put its membership at around 750,000 today. This compares with about 4,000 in the Methodist Church that did not have a place for such workings of the Holy Spirit back in 1910.[1] Many Methodists who blamed the devil for what happened in 1909 have since wondered out loud just on whose side the devil might really have been.[2]

During the same year, 1909, the first Pentecostal missionaries arrived in Argentina. They worked independently at the beginning, but in 1914 they affiliated with the Assemblies of God. Reinforcements were sent from the United States and Canada, and the gospel was proclaimed in Buenos Aires and other places. But in spite of dedication and hard work, over forty years of ministry had produced only 174 adult church members by 1951.[3]

The Pentecostal missionaries were downhearted. Much of their labor seemed to have been in vain. They prayed for something more. They needed a fresh and unusual outpouring of the Spirit of God. But discouragement grew, for nothing seemed to be happening.

Something was happening, however. In 1952

in Tallahassee, Florida, a forty-four-year-old evangelist named Tommy Hicks was conducting a series of meetings, when God sent him a vision.[4] As he prayed, a map of South America appeared vividly to him. The map was covered with a vast field of yellow grain, bent over and ready for the harvest. As Hicks contemplated the beautiful scene of grain waving under the noonday sun, the stalks of wheat suddenly began to change to human bodies, men and women with their hands raised high. They were crying out, "Come, Brother Hicks, come and help us!"

Hicks interpreted this as a Macedonian vision. From that moment he knew beyond the shadow of a doubt that God had some special task for him in South America. South America? He hardly knew a thing about that part of the world, but there was no mistaking the map he had seen. As he continued to pray, God gave him a message that he wrote in his Bible: "For two snows will not pass over the earth until thou shalt go to this land, for thou shalt not go by boat nor by land but as a bird, flying through the air shalt thou go."

Three months later, in Red Bluff, California, the vision was confirmed. In a pastor's home, after a successful evangelistic crusade, the pastor's wife while leading in prayer stretched out her hand toward Hicks and repeated the identical words of his message. He had not mentioned his vision to anyone, but when he showed the lady what had been written in his Bible previously, she broke down in tears.

As soon as he could, Tommy Hicks paid all his debts and made arrangements to travel to an unknown land. He had very little money, but suddenly he began to receive an astonishing amount of mail, much of which brought spontaneous contributions. Within ten days he had enough to purchase a one-way ticket to Buenos Aires, Argentina, with $47 left over. A group of friends saw him off at the Los Angeles International airport, adding a gift of $200 to his expense money.

"When I stop and think," Hicks now says, "how ridiculous it seemed, that I was going to a land that I did not know and people who did not know me—I could not even speak the language—and had only my ticket and $47. But within my soul I was at peace with God. . . ." [5]

On the last leg of the flight, after some fine meetings in Temuco, Chile, the name "Perón" kept coming to Hicks' mind. He had no idea what "Perón" meant, but he had a strange feeling that God was speaking to him. Hicks called the stewardess, and asked, "Do you know anyone around here by the name of Perón?" The stewardess looked rather startled, and said, "Yes, Mr. Perón is the President of Argentina."

Hicks' mandate was clear—God wanted him to talk to the President himself.

The missionaries he contacted when he arrived advised him against seeking an interview with the President. In the first place, they doubted whether he would be able to arrange it at all. But then, they feared that if he ever got near the President's office, he would run the risk of being arrested and sent to Tierra del Fuego, Argentina's equivalent to Siberia.

Undaunted, Hicks went anyway.

After some persistence, Hicks got into the office of the Minister of Religion, but that appeared to be as far as he was going. Perón could not handle any more visitors; in fact, the President of Panama was scheduled for an important state visit that day.

Then the minister's secretary came in limping. His left leg had turned black and blue, and the muscles had stiffened. The knee was badly swollen, and he asked permission to go home. Hicks suggested that they pray about it. The secretary scoffed and said, "If Jesus Christ were here Himself, He couldn't help this leg."

Tommy Hicks walked up to the man, knelt, and put his hands around the ailing knee. He prayed and asked Jesus to show His power. Hicks could feel the muscles begin to loosen. The secretary's eyes widened in astonishment—the pain had disappeared!

Hicks said to the dazed minister, "Can I see the President now?"

"I'll take you myself," he replied with a friendly grin.

God had prepared the way. Perón was cordial and warm. Toward the end of the interview he embraced Tommy Hicks, thanked him sincerely for his visit, and they prayed together. Perón then instructed his assistant to give Hicks whatever he asked for. The first request made and granted was the use of a large stadium and free access to the government radio and press.

Recent studies on the church in Argentina have revealed the crucial importance of the Tommy Hicks' campaign of 1954, not only for the Pentecostals, but also for all other churches which cooperated with the meetings. Arno Enns, who has written the standard church history for Argentina, calls the Hicks campaign "a sovereign breakthrough by God." [6] The influential book, *Latin American Church Growth* says, "Many Evangelicals in Argentina, whether or not they agree with Hicks' theology, admit that his meetings broke the back of the rigid Argentine resistance to the evangelical witness." [7]

Hicks preached for fifty-two days to an aggregate attendance of some two million. A Buenos Aires newspaper reported an attendance at the final meeting of 200,000. Although other denominations cooperated as well, the services were typically Pentecostal, with divine healing a prominent ingredient. All Evangelicals profited, but the Pentecostals particularly began a rapid period of growth which has made them the most numerous group of Protestants in Argentina today.

During that magic year of 1909, when the revival broke out in Chile and when the first Pentecostal missionaries went to Argentina, God was also working in the lives of one Italian and two Swedes in midwestern United States. He was going to use them to introduce the Pentecostal movement into Latin America's giant nation, Brazil.[8]

Louis Francescon, a humble, unassuming Italian immigrant, had received the baptism in the Holy Spirit and had spoken in tongues at William H. Durham's North Avenue Mission in Chicago in 1907. Moving among other Italians, Francescon planted churches (the denomination is now called Christian Church of North America) in California and Pennsylvania.[9] Then in 1909, he found himself under a "strong compulsion" to go to South America, a compulsion which he could explain in no way other than its being the direct leading of God.

It is well-known that other large groups of Italians had migrated to Argentina and Brazil, so when Francescon set forth on his first missionary journey (he made eleven in all), he spent a short time among the Italians in Buenos Aires. He then went to Sao Paulo, Brazil.

Sao Paulo had a "little Italy" colony of about 1,300,000 at that time, but Francescon did not know any of them. Praying that God would guide him, he sat down to relax on a park bench in one of the city's plazas. There he struck up a conversation with an Italian fellow from the state of Paraná and led him to Christ. The man invited him to his home in Plantina, where Francescon was successful in bringing the entire family of seven to Christ. They formed the nucleus of the first Pentecostal church in that area.

Back in Sao Paulo, Francescon made contact with a Presbyterian Church in the Brás district. He was invited to preach, which he did in Italian. His message moved many of the church members, and all went well until he brought up speaking in tongues. Some of the Presbyterians reacted very strongly against this, while others were warmly curious. Tensions developed to the point that the elders ordered Francescon out. He left, but so did several other church members who were attracted by the Pentecostal emphasis. They were sad, because they felt that God had sent Francescon as a prophet to stir up new life in the Presbyterian church. But the leaders did not agree, and the split occurred.

This new congregation became the mother church for the *Congregacao Crista no Brasil*. The Brás Presbyterian church numbers only a few hundred today, while the Pentecostal church has grown to thousands. As a whole, the *Congregacao Crista* has become the second largest church in Brazil, with over 500,000 communicant members today. Several of their church buildings seat crowds of 5,000.

The largest church in Brazil, estimated at about 1,500,000, is the Assemblies of God. In 1909 two Swedish immigrants, Gunnar Vingren and Daniel Berg, in an intimate prayer meeting in South Bend, Indiana, received a prophecy telling them to go to Pará. Pará? They had never heard of a place by that name. So they went to the public library and finally discovered that there was a state in Brazil called Pará.

They had no idea as to how they would get to Brazil, but in due time another prophecy came telling them to go to New York and look for a certain man at a certain place. Their available cash was just enough for the night train to New York. They found the man, and he provided them the exact amount of money needed to book third-class passage on a freighter to the city of Belém, capital of Pará.

They arrived in 1910, bewildered and exhausted. Their wool suits were hardly appropriate attire for one of the world's hottest tropical cities. They relaxed on a park bench, not knowing what to do next, but praying that God would guide them. He guided them first to a Methodist missionary, who introduced them to a friendly Baptist pastor who in turn provided them lodging in some rooms behind the church. All went well until they had learned sufficient Portuguese to begin to preach. Then their Pentecostal tendencies came to the surface, and serious tensions arose in the Baptist church. A small group finally left the Baptist church with Vingren and Berg and formed a new congregation. From it sprouted the Assemblies of God in Brazil.[10] The Belém church itself now counts over 30,000 members, including the circle of its own daughter churches in the immediate area.

The denomination they started now holds the distinction of being the largest Protestant church in all of Latin America.

The growth of the Protestant church in Latin America during this century has been one of the dramatic success stories of modern missions. Here is how it has mushroomed:

* In 1900 there were about 50,000 Protestants in Latin America.
* In the 1930's growth passed the 1,000,000 mark.
* In the 1940's it passed the 2,000,000 mark.
* In the 1950's it passed the 5,000,000 mark.
* In the 1960's it passed the 10,000,000 mark.
* Already in the 1970's it has passed the 20,000,000 mark.
* Some statisticians project something around 100,000,000 for 2000 A.D.

These statistics are heartwarming. With an annual growth rate of ten percent, the Protestant church in Latin America is increasing at a rate three times that of the population in general. This is particularly encouraging when you take into account that the population growth in Latin America is the highest of any continent in the world.

But these rough statistics need further refinement. Latin American Protestants are divided into literally hundreds of denominations. Are all these denominations growing at equal rates?

Until 1969 only imprecise data was available to answer this question. But in 1969 the exhaustive study called *Latin American Church Growth* was published. It took the authors, William Read (Presbyterian), Victor Monterroso (Bible Church), and Harmon Johnson (Assemblies of God) three years to collect, compile, and analyze the data. When this information was made available, one of the findings that surprised many observers was that 63.3 percent of all Latin American Protestants were Pentecostals of one kind or another. This proportion has undoubtedly increased since 1969, and is likely well above the two-thirds figure by now.

Because of the typical fragmenting nature of Pentecostal churches, statistics which would show the largest single church in a particular country are not always meaningful. But Pentecostals are either the largest church or the largest natural grouping of churches in Brazil, Argentina, Chile, Peru, Ecuador, Colombia, Panama, El Salvador, Honduras, and Mexico.

Whether you are a Pentecostal or not, you have to admit that the Pentecostals are doing something right in Latin America. No accusation by disgruntled non-Pentecostals of "proselytizing" or "sheep-stealing" or "worldliness" or "superficiality" or whatever charge might be leveled against Pentecostals will suffice to explain their phenomenal growth. There is much more to it than that. Rather than throwing stones, as some non-Pentecostals do, they should be asking, "What can we learn from the spiritual descendants of Hoover, Hicks, Francescon, Vingren, and Berg?"

The balance of this book will attempt to answer that question.

2

Endued with Power from on High

The basic dynamic behind Pentecostal growth in Latin America is the power of the Holy Spirit.

Some will respond—how simplistic! I agree. But it is simplistic only to the degree that it attempts to explain *everything*.

When churches grow, men and women are passing from death to life, from the power of Satan to the power of God. A phenomenon which the Bible calls the "new birth" is occurring. Theologians label it "regeneration."

Whether you're a Pentecostal or a Baptist or a Lutheran or a Presbyterian, if you believe the Bible, you will agree that the new birth is no human accomplishment. It is a miracle, a spiritual miracle that happens through the power of God Himself. This is what the Apostle John is trying to say when he writes about God's children, "who were born not of blood, nor of the will of the flesh, nor of the will of man, but of God." (Jn. 1:13)

Pentecostals will be the first to agree that the growth of their churches is due to the work of the Spirit of God, and not to human efforts. Hoover wrote, for example:

> I believe that the true secret of this whole thing is that we really and truly believe in the Holy Spirit— we *really* trust Him—we *really* honor Him—we *really* obey Him—we *really* give Him free rein—we *really* believe that the promise in Acts 1:4-5 and Joel 2:28-29 is for us . . .[1]

Attributing the conversions they see in their churches to the Holy Spirit, at times, however, leads some Pentecostals down a dangerous road. Some end up claiming, either in so many words or by their attitudes, that they have a corner on the Holy Spirit. Some might even lead you to think that they believe the Holy Spirit is working only in Pentecostal churches—He is not to be found in other churches. This misguided arrogance has turned some brethren against the Pentecostal movement in general, and it is a shame.

Anti-Pentecostalism is one of the most unfortunate aspects of the Latin American scene. Although it is not a Christian attitude, "The eye cannot say unto the hand, 'I have no need of you . . .'" (1 Co. 12:21), it is easy to see how it might have developed. Pentecostals themselves shoulder some of the blame for scorning their more traditional brethren. But non-Pentecostals generally are equally at fault for not being open to new workings of the Holy Spirit. The Methodist Church of Chile is Exhibit A—they simply could not believe that Hoover and the other brethren could really be acting according to the will of God.

Instead of learning something new from the Pentecostals, many traditional churches did their best to destroy or discredit the movement, particularly during the first half of our century. Pentecostals were frequently accused of "sheep stealing," since a significant number of Christians, once they had the option, decided to leave their sluggish churches and cast their lot with the Pentecostals, because that's where the action was.

Worse yet, they were even accused by some as being heretical. For many years one of the best-selling Spanish textbooks on false cults had parallel chapters on Jehovah's Witnesses, Mormons, Christian Science, Spiritism, *Pentecostalism*, and others. So little was the Pentecostal phenomenon understood in the churches that some harbored serious doubts as to whether Pentecostals could really be saved.

With a few exceptions, this attitude has now thawed all over Latin America. Pentecostals are regarded as brethren in Christ by almost all Latin American Evangelicals. And most Pentecostals no longer leave the impression that they are the only ones with the Holy Spirit.

But the non-Pentecostal churches still have a problem. They recognize the obvious fact that Pentecostal churches are growing a good deal more rapidly than most of the other kinds of churches. They ask themselves the question, why? They become even more frustrated when they put what is happening in theological terms, and come up against the possibility that somehow the Holy Spirit is able to work the miracle of regeneration more frequently in the Pentecostal churches than in their own. Instead of saying, "What can we do to clear the underbrush in our churches so that the Holy Spirit can work?" they often begin to rationalize their own fruitless activities theologically.

One of the theological rationalizations frequently stated is this: "The Pentecostals may get the quantity, but we are interested in quality." There is little biblical or theological soundness in this. Quality and quantity complement each other in church growth; they are not opposites. The highest quality churches in the New Testament were the ones, like the church at Thessalonica, that were active in sounding forth the Word of the Lord (1 Th. 1:8), and those to which the Lord added "day by day those who were being saved." (Ac. 2:47) One of the surest signs of a healthy church is its effectiveness in seeking and finding the stray sheep, and returning them to the Shepherd and Bishop of their souls (1 Pe. 2:25).

The other common theological rationalization has been called a "theology of search." Search theology claims that God is indifferent toward results. It piously "refuses to be tyrannized by statistics." Witness is defined not as bringing men and women to faith and repentance, but at best as just proclaiming the Good News whether anything happens or not, and at worst as whatever the church happens to be doing at the time. With a touch of good-natured irony, Donald McGavran describes search theology with these words: "the shepherds, going out to search for lost sheep, meet at the gate to announce that they do not intend to notice particularly how many are found." [2]

God, of course, notices how many are found. So do Latin American Pentecostals in general. Their evangelism is aggressive; their goal is to make disciples. They know and exercise the power of positive thinking. This is one reason why the Holy Spirit has been able to work in an extraordinary way through Pentecostal brethren. It may well be that He yearns to work just as powerfully through other churches, but finds Himself quenched (1 Th. 5:19) in many of them.

This brings us to the most important question in this chapter: How much of the Pentecostal success in Latin America can be traced to the Pentecostal *doctrine* of the Holy Spirit?

The answer to this very complex question is probably something like this: The Pentecostal doctrine of the Holy Spirit probably is somewhat less significant than Pentecostals like to think, and somewhat more significant than non-Pentecostals like to think.

Notice, we are not asking the question as to how important the Holy Spirit *Himself* is. This is not a point of debate. We are asking about the way Pentecostals articulate their belief in the Holy Spirit.

Just how do Pentecostals differ from other Evangelicals in their doctrine of the Holy Spirit? One of the differences is in degree, and the other is in kind.

The difference in degree simply means that Pentecostals tend to emphasize the Holy Spirit in their preaching, their worship, their conversation, their singing, and their writing more than other Evangelicals. Some criticize the Pentecostals for this emphasis on the grounds that too much stress on the Holy Spirit siphons off some of the glory that should go to Jesus Christ. They cite Jesus' words in John 16:14 in support: "[The Spirit] shall glorify Me; for He shall take of Mine, and shall disclose it to you."

Pentecostals agree that Jesus Christ needs to be glorified, but they believe that He is best glorified by a strong emphasis on the person and work of the Holy Spirit. In all fairness it should be mentioned that as far as I have been able to observe Pentecostal teaching and worship, Jesus Christ is honored no less in Pentecostal churches than He is in any other evangelical church in Latin America.

But the doctrine of the Spirit differs in kind also. The Pentecostal experience is central in Pentecostal churches. Called "baptism in the Spirit," this experience is usually considered as a blessing separate from and subsequent to conversion. According to the Pentecostal belief, conversion is something that happens to unbelievers, but the baptism in the Spirit is something that happens to believers. It is not impossible, they say, that a person could be baptized in the Spirit very soon after he is saved. It could come five minutes afterward, or five days, or five years. But most Pentecostals agree that, as on the day of Pentecost, it is accompanied by speaking in tongues (Ac. 2:4).

They are convinced that this baptism in the Spirit with the sign of tongues releases a spiritual power for Christian life and witness that other Christians do not have. Thousands of personal testimonies show that this is true in many lives. Whether it can be asserted as a universal theological truth is open to serious questions on both biblical and experiential grounds.

The temptation at this point is to digress. It is not the purpose of this book, however, to discuss the pros and cons of the Pentecostal doctrine of the Holy Spirit. Within the last two years at least a dozen excellent books on the subject have been published, some defending one side, some the other, and some in between. Our purpose is to ask whether this particular doctrine is directly related to the phenomenal growth of the Pentecostal church in Latin America.

On this score, the evidence indicates that, whereas doctrine undoubtedly has something to do with Pentecostal growth, it by no means is the only factor. It probably is not even the principal factor. As subsequent chapters will show, many things the Pentecostals are doing other than teaching a particular doctrine of pneumatology (theologese for the doctrine of the Holy Spirit) are contributing as much or more to their church growth in Latin America.

I want to stress this point since it is one of the reasons I am writing this book. As I will often repeat, I am convinced that many non-Pentecostal churches are missing a great opportunity for reaping the evangelistic harvest in Latin America because they are hung up precisely on this point. They think that in order to share the great blessing of seeing large numbers of unbelievers committing themselves to Christ, they have to become Pentecostals, meaning they have to agree with Pentecostal pneumatology.

I contend that they do not. Whereas it might

not hurt many of them to take a fresh look at their pneumatology, this is not nearly as important as learning many other lessons from the Pentecostals which will prove to be even more valuable than that.

Three evidences, above others, point to the fact that true-blue Pentecostal doctrine is not a consistent, across-the-board factor in rapid church growth.

1. First of all, not all Pentecostals agree with each other. It is questionable whether there really is anything like true-blue Pentecostal doctrine. The Methodist Pentecostal Church in Chile, mentioned in Chapter 1, for example, is highly regarded in both Pentecostal and non-Pentecostal circles. Since the days of Hoover, baptism in the Spirit has been an important feature of the church. But, unlike other Pentecostals, they do not think that speaking in tongues is an indispensable sign of this baptism.

Instead of speaking in tongues, some have manifested the baptism by dancing in the Spirit, or by uncontrollable joy or by increased courage and power in leading others to Christ or by other signs. Many speak in tongues, but it has not become the status symbol that some other Pentecostals seem to make it. In fact, a recent survey indicated that sixty percent of their pastors had never spoken in tongues.[3]

In spite of this deviation, the Methodist Pentecostal Church has grown at a very healthy rate through the years.

On another score, some researchers have found that speaking in tongues in Haiti does not set the Pentecostal apart from others nearly as much as the ceremony of burning Voodoo objects. The Haitian Pentecostal movement, thus, is not exactly a carbon copy of twin Chilean or Mexican counterparts.[4]

2. Secondly, it is a simple fact that some Pentecostals who hold the classic pneumatology are not growing rapidly. They are just as weak, just as ingrown, and just as unexciting as their neighbors who articulate their belief in the Holy Spirit in other ways. In Bolivia, for example, Pentecostals were only 7.5 percent of all Evangelicals when *Latin American Church Growth* was written. True, they came later than some other churches, but even so, they had not made an outstanding showing for two decades. By way of contrast, in Chile, the next country over, Pentecostals numberd 83 percent of all Evangelicals.[5]

If every single church which taught Pentecostal doctrine were growing, we would have to revise our conclusion. But uneven Pentecostal growth rates at least indicate that it is more complex than just that.

3. Some Pentecostals won't even want me to mention this third point. But it is true that by far the fastest growing church in Colombia is the United Pentecostal Church. The United Pentecostal Church is somewhat unorthodox because it baptizes, not in the name of the Father, the Son, and the Holy Ghost, but in the name of Jesus. Its nickname is "Jesus only," and more orthodox Pentecostals feel much the same about them as other Evangelicals felt about Pentecostals in general thirty years ago—they consider them as one of the false cults. They become very uncomfortable when the United Pentecostals refuse to dot the

i's and cross the t's of the Council of Nicea (the famous church council of 325 A.D. where the present doctrine of the trinity—three persons in one essence—was articulated and approved).

United Pentecostals, of course, don't agree. They preach salvation by the blood of Christ and can testify to multitudes of transformed lives as signs of people being born again. They believe in the Holy Spirit, in baptism in the Spirit, and in speaking in tongues. They consider themselves true Pentecostals, as their name implies. They are not Jehovah's Witnesses who deny the deity of Christ. And if anyone doubts their spiritual power, they could simply point to the following graph which compares their church growth to that of the next largest Pentecostal church, the Church of the Foursquare Gospel. The Foursquare is a more orthodox Pentecostal church.

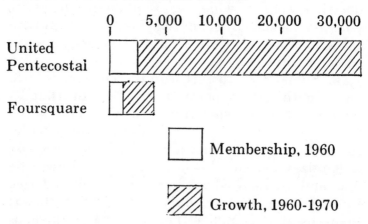

Source: Donald Palmer, *Growth of Pentecostal Churches in Colombia,* unpublished M.A. thesis (Deerfield: Trinity Evangelical Divinity School, 1972), p. 22.

The purpose in mentioning this is, of course, not to suggest that the United Pentecostals are growing *because* of their confusing "Jesus only" doctrine. I am a trinitarian, and I believe the Council of Nicea did a pretty fair job in articulating New Testament truth. My point is this: just as the United Pentecostals are growing in Colombia apparently because of non-doctrinal factors, Latin American Pentecostals in general also appear to be growing largely because of non-doctrinal factors. Almost all the remainder of this book will attempt to isolate and describe these factors.

Before we go on, however, let me stress two things.

First, I believe it is most helpful to look at Pentecostalism not as a well-established set of doctrines, but rather as a particular Christian life style. It is more a dynamic mood than a crystallized theology. You can tell Pentecostals more by what they do than by what they teach. Not all Pentecostals speak in tongues, but none forbid speaking in tongues. Not all Pentecostals believe in the Holy Spirit as a separate person in the Trinity, but all claim the power and authority of the Holy Spirit as a real person.

As we will see later, Pentecostals can even be members of non-Pentecostal churches. As a matter of fact, and this is highly important, it might be easier than we think for non-Pentecostal churches to "Pentecostalize" themselves without doctrinal compromise. In other words, non-Pentecostals might do well seriously to consider the possibility of behaving more like Pentecostals, even if they do not choose to believe like them.

Finally, it is a painful fact that sin can quench

— 39 —

the Spirit as effectively in a Pentecostal church as in a non-Pentecostal church. The devil goes around like a roaring lion, eager to devour every Christian he can. I have seen fine Pentecostal churches brought to the dust by sin. First Corinthians tells the story of a seemingly Pentecostal church where just that happened, but it could happen to any of us. This simply brings out once again the greater fact which was mentioned at the beginning of this chapter: when all is said and done, conversions, church growth, quality in the Christian life, and any other aspect of Christian experience is the product of the Holy Spirit.

God delights to use Christian men and women to accomplish His purpose in the world. But none of us can do it alone. In the twentieth century, just like the first, we will be effective only to the degree that we are "endued with power from on high." (Lk. 24:49)

3

Taking the Gospel to the People

If you go to Santiago, Chile, plan your trip over a weekend and spend Sunday afternoon and evening watching the Pentecostals in action. Their open-air meetings have become as much a part of Chilean local color as copper cream pitchers or Araucanian Indian artifacts.

You will have no difficulty in finding the "Canutos," as Chileans have nicknamed their Pentecostals after one of their early leaders. Just take a bus and get off somewhere around the railroad station at about five o'clock in the afternoon. Begin walking in almost any direction, and you will soon see a group of people on a street corner or in a plaza. Chances are they are Methodist Pentecostals from the big mother church, called the Jotabeche Church.

As you approach them, you will do well to carry a large Bible. That is like an admission ticket into the circle. If you don't have one, a brother or sister will most likely try to convert you on the spot. You will hear them singing and reciting Bible verses in unison from a block away.

When you get closer, you will see maybe ten guitars with long red ribbons streaming from them, three or four accordions, and a portable loudspeaker or two. The total group might number anywhere from thirty to a couple of hundred. After hymns and Scripture, one person will take the loudspeaker and begin to preach.

The speaker might be an experienced leader, or he may be a recent convert. So deeply do Chilean Pentecostals believe in street meetings that a virtual requirement for a legitimate conversion experience is that you agree to go out on the street the Sunday after your decision and give your testimony as to what God did in your life.

This procedure has two distinct benefits. It first helps the new believer to cement his faith in Christ and his relationship to the body. He may be rather inarticulate and scared half to death to speak in public, but this ultimately helps him to feel like an active participant in the mission of the church in the world. As he speaks, his companions are praying him through, and at the same time they are making him feel very warm toward the other members of the group.

The second benefit is that, in spite of lack of training and a stuttering delivery, the message gets through—possibly more so than it might for a polished, professional minister. The testimony carries with it a high degree of credibility, since the speaker can so readily identify with the listeners who come from the same social class, dress like he does, and understand his way of speaking Spanish.

When the meeting on one corner is finished, the spectators are not given a piece of Christian literature and invited to come to church "sometime" as they often are by less effective street preachers. Instead, they are urged to "come right along with us to church *tonight*." Individuals will move out and be sure each spectator is gently persuaded to join the crowd.

The crowd will slowly move one or two blocks nearer the church, and stop for another brief meeting. This continues, meeting after meeting, until they have only enough time to march to the church and arrive at about seven o'clock, bringing the new visitors with them.

They meet others as they approach the church. About thirty of these open-air evanglistic groups will have been working in the immediate vicinity of the Jotabeche Church. They fill the streets. Often traffic has to be detoured. The church officers step outside to greet the street preaching teams as they arrive and file into the sanctuary, singing loudly as they go in.

Many non-Pentecostals think street preaching is old-fashioned. Some regard it as a public spectacle that cheapens the gospel. They may not use these words, but they say, in effect, "Singing and yelling out there on the street is beneath my dignity." Some braver souls may even have tried it on occasion, but failed because of inexperience or some other reason. From that they tend to generalize, claiming that "Street preaching doesn't work, anyway."

Does it really work? The members of the Jotabeche Church think it does. If you need proof, they will simply point to their new sanctuary. The former one, on Jotabeche Street, had a seating capacity of only 5,000, so after many years of over- flow crowds standing out in the street, they decided to rebuild. Their new church, on the same corner, but facing out on Santiago's main thoroughfare, seats 16,000!

Those who analyze what they are doing theo- logically will tell you that they are only obeying Jesus' commands to go and preach the gospel to every creature. But they stress the word *go* in con- trast to many others who expect unbelievers to *come.* They are aggressive in their evangelism while slower growing churches are invariably more passive. They untiringly proclaim the mes- sage of salvation to the lost, but they are not satis- fied with proclamation only. They believe in per- suading their unbelieving friends to commit their lives to Christ and become responsible members of His church.

This last phrase, "responsible members of His church," is a key concept in unlocking the secrets of Pentecostal growth. To a very high degree, Pentecostals are church-centered, and this in- creases their effectiveness.

By "church-centered," I do not mean that they are ingrown and introverted—just the opposite! They know that Christ has commanded them to "make disciples," and they also know that dis- ciples are made from those out there in the world. If Pentecostals were centripetal (inward-moving), they wouldn't grow. They are, instead, centrifugal (outward-moving), intent on meeting unbelievers on their own ground, and there persuading them to become disciples of Jesus. They do not expect the people to come to the gospel; they diligently take the gospel to the people.

But at that point they do not make the mistake that others who are not so church-centered make. They are not content to see a newborn baby left out in the street. He needs spiritual care, the milk of the Word (1 Pe. 2:2), which he will not get in the street, but in the church. The lambs that are found must be brought into the fold where the shepherds can watch over them, heal their wounds, and help them to grow. They are not to be left in the ravines where the wild beasts will devour them.

Pentecostals are usually proud of their church. This is why they so often seem uninterested in participating in city-wide or nation-wide interdenominational crusades. Their seeming aloofness is not ordinarily due to any lack of love or respect for their brethren in other denominations as much as it is to an intuitive knowledge that the very nature of interdenominational evangelism often separates it too much from the local church.

It is a widely acknowledged fact that one of the weaknesses of mass, interdenominational evangelism has been what is called "follow up." Follow up means getting the people who make decisions into the churches. Some regard follow up as a separate step which comes after evangelism itself, but this is a fallacy all too common in evangelistic strategy. It is a trap that Pentecostals do not generally fall into. Some brethren have unwisely set up programs designating this year for evangelism and next year for follow up. Or others invite a professional evangelist for a week of evangelism, and intend to "follow up" after he leaves.

An even more severe fallacy is to "leave the

— 45 —

follow up to God." Evangelism to some is simply getting people to sign a decision card, or to pray to receive Christ, then moving on, hoping against hope that somehow the lambs will be found and taken into the fold. Statistics show that it doesn't usually happen like that.

This is why Pentecostals stress "making disciples" rather than "getting decisions." The Great Commission includes two activities along with "going" and "making disciples," namely, "baptizing" and "teaching" (Mt. 28:19-20). Jesus did not separate follow up from evangelism. He included them all in the same package of "making disciples." According to Acts 2, disciples continually devoted themselves to the apostles' teaching, to fellowship, to breaking of bread, and to prayers. In other words, converts should stick on as responsible church members.

Research shows that evangelistic programs can be attractive, flamboyant, heavily-financed, expertly staffed, strongly prayed for—but relatively fruitless if they are not properly related to the local churches as an integral part of the program, not as an afterthought.

One of Latin America's top evangelistic preachers once brought this up to me in a personal conversation. He was concerned, he said, as to why his city-wide crusades would produce so many apparent decisions for Christ, but that so little fruit would remain. He was not a Pentecostal, incidentally, although he believed in the baptism in the Spirit and had received it himself. This again points out that his lack of evangelistic fruit was not a doctrinal problem. I was equally concerned, because one of my students had researched several evangelistic crusades in Cochabamba, Bolivia, and had shown statistically that they had been surprisingly ineffective in "adding to the *church* such as should be saved." (Ac. 2:47)

My friend had just held the first of a week-long series of evangelistic meetings in a rented auditorium. The building had been filled, and some fifty people had responded to the invitation by coming forward. But he knew and I knew that (apart from some believers in the group who were rededicating their lives to God) very few of those who came forward would be found in the Cochabamba churches six months hence.

He belonged to an evangelistic association which stressed the value of interdenominational crusades. By nature, it was not church-centered. I suggested to him that this might be one of the problems. Holding the meetings in such a non-church building as this rented auditorium did not help the new converts to associate their decision with the local church. Neither did the instruction.

I asked the evangelist, "When you finished leading the people who came forward in the sinner's prayer, what did you counsel them to do next?"

He replied, "Read their Bibles, pray regularly, and tell someone else about their decision."

In my opinion there is a mistake here, a mistake that most Pentecostals would not make. There is nothing wrong with Bible reading, praying, and witnessing—they are all beautiful Christian virtues. But the evangelist's instructions to the newborn babes left out another Christian virtue that *at that particular moment of their experience,* was more important than all three put together—becoming a committed member of a local body of believers, a church.

This cannot be overstressed. Jesus included

"baptizing them" as a part of the Great Commission. Baptism in its simplest definition is merely the rite of incorporation into the body of Christ in its local and visible form. When you join a church, you commit yourself not only to God, but to other believers. The members of the body encourage and nourish one another. When converts are added to the church, they are likely to go on for Christ.

Christians differ in their opinions as to the form of baptism and who should be baptized. In Latin America, most Protestants insist on rebaptizing converted Catholics, but some accept Catholic baptism. Even Pentecostals do not all agree with each other. In Chile the Methodist Pentecostals have retained enough "Methodism" to continue baptizing infants, unlike most other Latin American Pentecostals.

One of Buenos Aires' largest and most rapidly growing churches stresses incorporation so much that the pastor was once suspected of holding the doctrine of "baptismal regeneration." He did not let this intramural quarrel (Pentecostals were on both sides, incidentally) stifle his evangelistic effectiveness, however.

Members of his church witness constantly, and then bring those who are interested to church on Sunday evening. After the singing, the pastor invites all visitors to stand to receive a gift from the church, and the deacons distribute New Testaments to them. He then tells them that, since they came to find out the meaning of the gospel and how to become a Christian, they should not stay in the main sanctuary. "My message will be directed to believers, not to you," he says. He then instructs them to move into another room where some laymen will explain to them how to become Christians.

Once they are in the other room, with some of the church's top personal evangelists, you could correctly predict that the percentage of decisions is high. But along with this, the percentage of those who become disciples, who are "continually devoting themselves to the apostles' teaching, and to fellowship, to the breaking of bread and to prayer" is high also. Why? Chiefly because they are immediately associated with the church. There is no difference between evangelism and follow up there.

Three things tie them closely to the church:

1. They make their decision right there in the church. The church, in a sense, is the spiritual delivery room for their new birth. Church members, not a visiting preacher from outside, are the obstetricians.

2. Without apology, they are told that if they are sincere in committing themselves to Christ, they must immediately obey His command to be baptized. To them, baptism is not something optional that Christians may or may not like to do six months, or two years, or ten years from now. Christ is Lord, and His commandments must be obeyed now. They feel that if an inquirer says, "I want to believe in Christ, but I do not want to follow Him in baptism," there is a real question as to the validity of his decision.

3. The new babes in Christ do not go home alone. A church member is assigned to each one, and accompanies him to his home. In the usual Latin American fashion, the visitor is often invited

into the home, offered a cup of coffee, and meets the family. Before he goes, he makes arrangements to take the new believer, and his family if possible, to church the next Sunday. This helps seal his incorporation into the body.[1]

Church-centeredness, then, is important to these Pentecostals in Buenos Aires, just as it is to those in Santiago, Chile. It was also important in a highly significant mass evangelistic crusade in Guayaquíl, Ecuador, in 1962.

Missionaries of the Church of the Foursquare Gospel arrived in Guayaquíl in 1957.[2] By 1962 they had a small church of thirty members, hardly growing at all. Billy Graham had recently completed a dramatic crusade in the capital of Quito and Guayaquíl, Ecuador's largest city, wanted some of the same. Since Billy Graham himself couldn't come, the churches banded together and held their own crusade. They worked for six months and spent thousands of dollars for a six-day evangelistic campaign in June, 1962. The maximum attendance was 6,000 and measurable results practically zero!

Even though the preacher was not a Pentecostal, the Foursquare Church cooperated with the crusade and suffered disappointment along with the rest. They then began a twenty-four-hour-a-day prayer chain, asking the Lord for something better. The Foursquare people took the initiative for another crusade later that year, invited a Pentecostal preacher, and sought the cooperation of the other denominations. When the time came, not only did the other churches refuse to cooperate, but some non-Pentecostal leaders even tried to discredit the whole effort and discourage attendance.

The Foursquare brethren were saddened by this turn of events, but they need not have been. It was without a doubt a blessing in disguise, for it forced the crusade to be more church-centered than it might have been.

God used many different dynamic forces to bring abundant fruit through this evangelistic effort in Guayaquíl. They will be mentioned in due time. But the point we are making here is that when people made their decisions to follow Christ, there was no question at all about church membership—they were expected to become members of the Foursquare Church. Thus, when the crusade was completed after six weeks, a public baptism was held. A remarkable crowd of 30,000 showed up to witness the baptism of 1,500 converts, all of whom had received instruction and who were willing to commit themselves to the local church as well as to Christ.

For the next four years the momentum continued. An average of sixty-five new converts were baptized each month for those four years. By 1966 the Foursquare had forty-two churches with a membership of over 4,000!

How those forty-two new churches were established is another story, It will be told in the following chapter.

4

Mothers and Daughters—
Church Reproduction

When the Foursquare brethren in Guayaquíl, Ecuador, launched their evangelistic crusade in 1962, they were, like many of us, "ye of little faith." They expected some results, but none would have dared to predict that in a period of six weeks one struggling church of thirty members would become seven churches with 1,500 members.

The Holy Spirit gave them special wisdom, however, when they began to take notice that God was doing something unusual in their midst. Attendance soared from less than 1,000 the first night to 10,000 the second night, to 20,000 during the second week, and to over 30,000 before they had finished. Meetings were held in a large, open field, with listeners standing throughout the two to three-hour service. When people began to respond to the invitations, committing their lives to Jesus Christ, the brethren in charge immediately began wisely to build "follow up" right into the crusade.[1]

The crusade lasted six weeks, not six days. This extended period of time has proven valuable time and again in concentrated evangelistic efforts in Latin America, although it occurs much too infrequently. But, as the Pentecostals in Ecuador can tell us, it provides opportunity not only to win people to Christ, but also to give them their first spiritual food and help them grow in their tender faith.

As soon as they realized that a substantial number of people had been converted, the leaders changed the order of service of the crusade meetings. At the beginning of the meetings they introduced one half hour of basic Bible instruction for new believers. The evangelist's wife took charge of this, and by the time the six weeks were over the converts were well aware of what the Christian life was all about. Of them, 1,500 were ready for baptism in water.

But what do you do with 1,500 baptized Christians? The Foursquare Church wouldn't hold a fraction of them. Furthermore, they came from all over Guayaquíl, Ecuador's largest city, and travel would be a problem in getting them together regularly. The inescapable conclusion was that several different churches had to be started around the city.

This was a problem, especially since it hadn't been anticipated. No careful, strategic plans had been laid. But the Foursquare missionary, Roberto Aguirre, was courageous enough to do just about the only thing he could do. He called together the Sunday School teachers, a typical group of busy lay Christians who were struggling with the burden of making a living for their families but desirous of serving God in some way. Aguirre described the problem to them. He suggested that the only way to care for the new believers was to start more churches. The Sunday School teachers were with him.

Then he tossed out the bomb. "You people," he said, "are going to be the pastors!"

Eyes widened and mouths dropped. It was one thing to teach Bible for an hour on Sunday morning to a small group of eighth graders. It was something far different to be responsible for a sizable church in the city of Guayaquíl. But as they prayed together, their faith grew, and they trusted God for whatever was necessary to care for the new believers and continue their efforts to win not only Guayaquíl, but all of Ecuador, for Christ.

Seven new churches began immediately. The young believers not only received spiritual food and straightened out their lives, but they began to win other friends and neighbors. One of the interesting sidelights of the whole revival occurred, of all places, in the city marriage license bureau. The officials were so flooded with men and women desirous of straightening out their twisted family situations that they completely ran out of printed marriage license forms and had to close the office until new ones were printed!

Through a combination of the force of circumstances and direction that could only have come from God Himself, the Foursquare Church in Guayaquíl learned a lesson that careful research has proved to be valid, not only in Latin America, but in almost any part of the world. Church growth is usually rapid where not only individuals are being won to Christ, but where simultaneously *churches are being multiplied.* This was continued in Ecuador, so that in four years the one church in Guayaquíl had become forty-two churches all over the republic.

It also happened in Colombia. The rapidly growing United Pentecostal Church has risen to first place numerically among Colombia's Protestant churches largely on this principle. According to Donald Palmer, who has written a full survey of Colombian Pentecostal churches, this is a definite pattern.[2] Churches which are growing rapidly in Colombia are precisely those which are actively multiplying local churches. Between 1960 and 1970, the Assemblies of God planted fifty new churches, the Panamerican Mission thirty-six new churches, the Foursquare forty-five, and the United Pentecostal an incredible 357. These four healthy churches are all Pentecostal, and they all practice the principle of church multiplication.

In contrast, the Cumberland Presbyterian Church, which has been in Colombia longer than any of the Pentecostal churches, is one of Colombia's slowest-growing churches. In that same ten-year period (1960-1970) they planted only one new church. But it is revealing to notice that the Cumberland Presbyterians have the highest average membership per local church. This brings up another principle, crucial for healthy church growth.

We do well to recognize that every church has an optimum size. Big churches are good and have many advantages, but they should realize that, like most mothers, they have an optimum weight. When they pass that they get fat, unattractive, and inefficient. Rather than allowing such a process to set in, the best strategy for churches (although not always for mothers!) is to have children. In Colombia, and in other places in Latin America, Pentecostals practice this principle, while others, like the Cumerland Presbyterians, do not seem to recognize the optimum size factor. This is one reason why, in Colombia, all Pentecostal churches are growing at a rate of over 150 percent per decade, while Cumberland Presbyterians are growing at only 44 percent.[3]

Perhaps the most dramatic illustration of Pentecostal church reproduction is found in the Brazil for Christ Church in Sao Paulo, Brazil.[4] This is the church led by Manoel de Melo, one of the best known Pentecostal leaders not only in Latin America but in the world.

Under de Melo's leadership, the Brazil for Christ Church is just completing construction of a sanctuary which will seat no less than 25,000 worshipers. He is probably not exaggerating when he calls it the "biggest church in the world." While construction of the huge edifice is progressing, the congregation has been meeting in what will eventually be the entrance hall. This seats well over 5,000 people. A friend of mine, staring in surprise when he first saw the vastness of the foyer, asked the caretaker how many pews were there. "I don't really know," he replied, "we ordered a mile and a half!"

Unless you know the system beforehand, even more surprising than the gigantic building is the size of the congregation that meets on Sunday morning. It numbers perhaps one hundred! You immediately ask, "Where are the five thousand?"

The five thousand meet on Thursday and Saturday nights, but on Sunday they are out where active Christians are supposed to be, according to Manoel de Melo. They are back in their neighborhoods winning new people to Christ and gathering them together in daughter churches. The big building is the mother, an active reproducer. In fact, she might hold the world's record for spiritual offspring. In the capital area of Sao Paulo alone a total of 1,496 new churches and congregations have been planted by enthusiastic members of the Brazil for Christ Church. Of them, 136 are fully organized churches (minimum requirement for organization is 100 baptized members), with twenty-five counting membership of over 1,500 each.

Statistics are not easy to keep up with in such a skyrocketing movement, but according to a very careful estimate made by an expert researcher, Brazil for Christ nationwide probably has about 4,000 organized churches, 250,000 baptized members, and a community of one million.[5] By any accounting, this is remarkable church growth for a movement only seventeen years old.

Manoel de Melo was from his childhood an effective evangelist. He began exercising his gift at about eleven years of age and has not let up since. He has spent the best part of a lifetime actively taking the gospel out to the people on the streets, in the plazas, in stadiums, or in tents. He never believed in sitting back and waiting for people to come to him. He characterizes his own ministry as a huge "fishing net," and rejoices at the multitudes of spiritual fish that God has given him over the years.

For many years, de Melo was content to let other Brazilian evangelical churches handle the "follow up," but this led to the problem that most evangelists not related to churches inevitably face. The distance between the sawdust trail and the communion table is greater than many evangelists imagine, and when they discover how much the spiritual fallout really amounts to they become frustrated. Manoel de Melo came to that place in 1955, and he decided to see that his converts got better care. He now says, "Brazil for Christ is a movement that plants churches . . . . Preaching itself is not enough. We have to preach, but we also have to teach."

The average organized church in the movement has ten small congregations that it has started and is responsible for. In other words, the Brazil for Christ Church is not only a mother, but in seventeen years is already a grandmother and a great-grandmother.

Some might think that, whereas it is easy for big city churches to go over ten blocks or so and find enough people to form the nucleus of a new daughter church, it is much more difficult to do the same thing in a rural situation. The Assemblies of God in Bolivia, however, are practicing church reproduction out in the country areas of Bolivia's windswept 13,000-foot Altiplano. Their missionary, Bruno Frigoli, is currently heading up the third year of a program called "Each-church-one-church-in-one-year."

Bolivian Pentecostal leaders have agreed to set as a measurable goal the planting of a new church every year. They realize they might not fully be able to accomplish their goal, but they are thinking church growth in a positive and optimistic way. Attractive certificates have been printed, one for each year, and churches are working to earn a string of certificates to hang on their walls. Whenever a daughter church is formed and organized (in this case ten baptized believers are required for the nucleus), the mother church gets the certificate signed by denominational officers.

The United States mission is helping some financially in establishing the new churches. The Aymara Indians of the Altiplano are, generally speaking, poor farmers, many still living only on the margin of the money economy. Yet they have found that having a church building is a great help in establishing their testimony in a new village or rancho. So when a new church is organized, the believers there are encouraged to get a piece of ground, make their own adobe bricks, and build the walls of the church building.

Before the mission will step in, they must also put on the first half of the galvanized tin roof. The mission will then pay for the roofing for the second half, buy the church a supply of literature, and furnish a mule or a bicycle for the pastor who takes charge, so he can move on to the next village to help plant a new church.

At the end of 1970 the Bolivian assemblies had only twenty churches. During 1971, thirty new ones were planted, making a total of fifty. Each one of the fifty was to plant a new church in 1972. In January of 1973 a total of 104 churches reported! The rate of growth for the Assemblies of God in Bolivia has increased tremendously through multiplication of churches. How long this pace can continue is anybody's guess, but the Bolivian Christians are not contemplating returning to their former pattern of sluggish growth.

The largest denomination in Latin America is the Assemblies of God of Brazil, as has already been mentioned. The Brazilians make full use of the mother-daughter pattern of church reproduction, and they have it well developed.[6]

There are over 200 large mother church complexes throughout the country. Each forms the nucleus of an evangelistic circle which radiates out like ripples on a millpond. The name they use for the mother church is "ministry." Smaller "ministries" number 500 or more, while the larger ones can go to 20,000, 30,000, or even 40,000 members, as in the case of the Madureira Church in Rio de Janeiro.

The mother church is responsible for every member of the Assemblies of God in its geographical area, until a new "ministry" breaks off and takes charge of a separate area. This dynamic process of decentralization works continually and keeps the entire denomination throbbing with vitality. The mother-daughter system has played a key role in swelling membership in the Brazilian Assemblies of God to around 1,500,000.

In describing the Brazilian Assemblies of God, Read, Monterroso, and Johnson make this revealing comment: "Restructuring often occurs as new dynamic leaders emerge and sometimes clash with the older leaders." [7] Their statement brings up another quite typical aspect of Latin American

Pentecostal church growth which some call "growth by splitting."

No one will say that church splits are intrinsically good. They frequently involve nasty quarrels and even legal hassles. Often they leave broken hearts and permanent enmities behind. Nevertheless, God promises that "all things work together for good to them that love God." (Rom. 8:28) Strangely enough, church splits among Pentecostals have frequently resulted in accelerated growth for both sides of the split. One might even wonder how the providence of God operates in many of these cases. Perhaps if the churches themselves do not plan for and execute amicable church reproduction, God will allow circumstances to develop which will cause the churches to reproduce anyway.

Since we live in what might be called the "ecumenical age" it is not stylish to attribute any good at all to something as unecumenical as church division, but this does not seem to bother many Pentecostals. In fact, according to historian J. B. A. Kessler, two of Chile's top Pentecostal leaders "do not share the horror for church division which is usually felt in ecumenical circles. In fact both believe that division has helped the astonishing growth of the Pentecostal churches in Chile more than it has hindered it." [8]

This has happened frequently in the Methodist Pentecostal Church. Back in 1946 an aspiring and highly gifted leader, Enrique Chávez, was coming up through the ranks, but the powers that be did not see eye to eye with many of his ideas. He was a restless man and did not appreciate being inhibited in his actions. He had gathered a substantial following by then. One thing led to another, and Chávez and his group split off from the Methodist Pentecostal Church to form the new Pentecostal Church of Chile. Within only ten years, Chávez had built a huge mother church in Curicó which some have likened to a "basilica." Twenty-six daughter churches and 100 others in formation were flourishing.[9] Chávez now claims over 60,000 members.

In 1952 it happened again. This time Victor Pavéz participated in the splinter group. Within ten years the new "Pentecostal Church Mission" had grown to eighteen churches with a membership of 10,000.[10] After a tedious study, Kessler concludes that the Methodist Pentecostal Church has seen fourteen splinter groups move away since the days of Hoover.[11] But, although there have been many painful incidents connected with these splits, they do not seem to have flagged evangelistic effectiveness either of the mother or of her rebellious daughters.

Biologically speaking, the cells in a healthy body are in a continuous process of division and multiplication. When the body of Christ is healthy, this will occur also. Effective evangelism not only seeks to win individuals and families and peoples to Christ, but to plant new churches as frequently as possible. There is nothing particularly Pentecostal about the mother-daughter church pattern. Any church can learn it and put it into practice. Pentecostals in general are doing a magnificent job of it in Latin America, and that is one of the reasons they are reaping such a large proportion of the harvest in those fields which God has whitened.

5
Sowing the Seed on Fertile Soil

The "Parable of the Sower" is found in the Bible in Matthew 13, Mark 4, and Luke 8. Curiously, it is one of the least understood parables in the New Testament in spite of the ample space that biblical writers have given it. But seen in proper perspective, it provides us the key to unlock what, in my opinion, may well be the most important factor in the analysis of Pentecostal growth in Latin America. I must confess, however, that this is not a particularly profound observation since church growth research worldwide has shown that *wherever* churches are growing the principle is being applied.

Exactly what is this principle?

It emerges when you attempt to interpret the parable as a farmer would. Today's urban-oriented people have a harder time doing that, perhaps, than did Jesus' disciples who were brought up in a rural setting. When farmers hear anything about sowing and harvesting, they immediately evaluate what is being said in terms of what I call "the vision of the fruit." When all is said and done, the thing that ultimately matters to any farmer is the fruit.

The parable involves a farmer who sowed seed on four kinds of soil. Whether they were separate fields or whether they were all parts of the same field makes no difference. Three of the soils did not produce fruit, but the other did. This is the best place to start in order to understand how the parable relates to church growth, or as Jesus put it, hearing "the word of the kingdom." (Mt. 13:19)

What was the factor that made only one out of four fields produce fruit?

It was not the sower, nor the method, nor the seed, nor the climate. The variable factor was the soil. The seed of the Word of God, like wheat or barley, will produce fruit only when it is wisely sown on fertile soil. No matter how good the seed is, or how dedicated the sower, nothing will grow if the seed falls on a hard roadside. Even prayer will not produce fruit from seed sown on barren ground, any more than prayer will cause oak trees to produce figs.

Some undoubtedly will feel uncomfortable with this emphasis. But before rejecting it, they should prayerfully look at the parable once more with farmer's eyes. The vision of the fruit will help them to see the principle of sowing seed on fertile soil both in its agricultural and its spiritual application.

God wants fruit. He wants the whitened fields reaped and the sheaves brought to the barn (Mt. 9:37-38). He is not willing that one should perish, but that all should come to repentance (2 Pe. 3:9). Preaching the gospel should bear fruit for eternity. It should make disciples, and thus fulfill God's will as expressed in the Great Commission.

Sowing the seed on barren soil has, unfortunately, become a habit for some missions. Year after year missionaries and evangelists "sow in tears" but they somehow never seem to "reap in joy" (Ps. 126:5), and thus they miss the blessing. As Haggai says, "Ye have sown much, but harvest little." (Hag. 1:6) Years of work sometimes produce a visible fig tree (Lk. 13:6-9), but one which bears no fruit. Since it is painful to cut it down, the "work" continues year after year whether it is fruitful or not.

Some missionaries even come to the point where they attempt to justify barrenness theologically, declaring that it may not be God's will after all that the preaching of the gospel bring men and women to repentance and faith. They thus become addicted to fruitlessness, and are to be pitied.

Fruitlessness, as we have seen, is not a characteristic of Latin American Pentecostals in general. They have found fertile soil, they sow seed there in abundance, and they joyfully reap a harvest. What is this fertile soil? In simple terms it is the *proletariat.*

All peoples in Latin America are not equally responsive to the gospel. Some constitute barren soil, as years of hard work and experimentation have shown. But the working classes, the disinherited masses, the migrant farmers, the squatters on the fringes of the cities, the poor and oppressed—the proletariat—have proved, in country after country, to be Latin America's fertile soil in the second half of the twentieth century. These are the people, generally speaking, that you find in the Pentecostal churches in Latin America.

Sociologists such as Emilio Willems[1] and Christian Lalive[2] who have studied Pentecostalism from their professional perspective, invariably comment on the proletarian nature of the Pentecostal churches. Without using the term, such writers provide accurate pointers toward identifying Latin America's fertile soils. In particular, peoples found in the areas of new urbanization and industrialization are receptive to the gospel. In the rural areas Willems found some receptive and some resistant. For example, peasants still under the old hacienda system where the Catholic land owner ruled with an iron hand were least receptive to the Protestant message. Free farmers were only moderately receptive. But those who had been uprooted and relocated in new agricultural areas were found to be highly receptive.[3]

Soils like these are made fertile by the providence of God. There is little way to explain varying degrees of receptivity among peoples without a strong belief in the sovereignty of God. He is known as the Lord of the harvest (Mt. 9:38). Men can sow and men can water, but only God can cause the growth (1 Co. 3:6-7). Man's chief responsibility in evangelistic work is to discern the hand of God in preparing soil or ripening harvests and to move in, under the power of the

Holy Spirit, to sow the seed and gather the sheaves.

Apparently God was at work in just that way in Chile back in the days of the great Pentecostal revival under Hoover, described in chapter one. God used visions and other means to inform His people of His work and will. But when Lalive describes the event from a modern sociologist's point of view, he sees it like this:

> The schism which divided the Methodist Episcopal Church and gave birth to a Chilean Pentecostalism was the result of the opposition between a middle-class ecclesiastical hierarchy, dominated by foreign influence, and the body of believers who were nationals of the lower classes . . .[4]

In plainer language, God had prepared the lower class in Chile for receiving the gospel, but the established Methodist church was not prepared to move in that direction with the aggressive evangelistic program that would bring multitudes of working people into their churches. To think of receiving large numbers of that kind of people was undoubtedly repugnant to many of the middle-class Methodists, although they probably would not have wanted to admit it. It is much easier to react against speaking in tongues and baptisms of fire on the grounds of being "anti-Methodist and anti-biblical" than it is to admit any kind of class prejudice.

Notice how important the missionary attitude was. Methodists were "dominated by foreign influence," according to Lalive. Further examination, however, will show that the "foreignness" of the missionaries was not the chief problem, at least not nearly as much the social class that the Methodist missionaries belonged to. A very large percentage of missionaries to Latin America have come from the middle class of United States or British countries, where the middle class is large. They are typically well-educated and have good manners. This is true not only of Methodists but also of Presbyterians and Baptists and members of the Latin America Mission.

Many missions demand a high degree of cultural and educational polish from their candidates, some even requiring both college and seminary. These are good qualities, but they do not particularly incline a person toward the lower classes. When such missionaries arrive in Latin America, they find a very small middle class, but still their natural identification is there. Sometimes they discover only too late that they have been assiduously sowing the seed in unproductive soil.

Pentecostalism has traditionally been a religion of the masses in contrast to the classes, even in the affluent countries. Missionaries from Pentecostal churches find identification with the Latin American masses a natural thing. Those from the more traditional denominations and missions have had an unfortunate tendency to regard Pentecostal missionaries with a degree of contempt because they were not seminary educated people, and many did not even have a Bible Institute diploma. But when all is said and done, the lack of skills in Hebrew, Greek, and epistemology may have been more than compensated for by the inherent ability to identify with the proletariat.

Like begets like. Middle-class missionaries often theorized that their ministry to the middle class would eventually win more of the lower classes. This has not occurred, however, either in Latin America or in other parts of the world. Religious movements in general move from the lower classes up, rather than *vice versa.*

Pentecostals might not have articulated this in such a way, but their social position placed them, predictably, in the midst of the lower class on the mission field. Growth began here, but due to the combination of what McGavran calls "redemption and lift"[5] their influence was also eventually felt in the middle class. Reports of an informal survey in Panama, for example, indicate that the Foursquare Church there now counts more well-educated professionals in its membership than the Methodist Church.

The "redemption and lift" factor operates when lower-class people are converted, and because of their improved moral life they begin to rise up the social ladder. This can be very detrimental to evangelistic effectiveness if, through it, people lose contact with their friends, neighbors, and relatives. It could have harmed Latin American Pentecostals if they had all risen rapidly to middle class status and lost contact with the proletariat.

But this did not happen. The Pentecostal churches have been growing so rapidly that a newly-converted first generation of members continues to flood in. This first generation is not particularly concerned with developing "respectability." Their children often are, however, and some of them even leave Pentecostalism to join what they consider (ironically because of the advantages they have received from their redeemed Pentecostal parents) more "respectable" churches.

For example, eighty percent of Chilean Pentecostal pastors are first generation Christians. Lalive comments on this, saying, ". . . more than half a century after its foundation, Pentecostalism is still in the first-generation period, and may be so for a long time to come." [6] This statement forces us to look toward the future.

Will the most fertile field for future growth in the churches in Latin America continue to be the lower classes? The general consensus is that they will. Australian Methodist Alan Walker says, "That Pentecostalism is touching the poorer millions of Latin America is of deep significance, . . . There is no future for any movement which fails to stir the masses." [7] Pentecostalism will undoubtedly continue to grow as long as it maintains its contact with the masses and thus continues to sow the gospel seed on fertile soil.

This has much to say to middle class missions and churches. As evangelistic strategy is planned for the future in Latin America, the vision of the fruit should be uppermost. Read, Monterroso, and Johnson, in their hard-hitting chapter, "Guidelines for Strategy," make this remarkable statement:

> While the Church is, of course, dedicated to reaching all men, regardless of their class or position, she should concentrate special attention on the masses who are receptive. The future of the Church lies with the common people. [8]

Whether this advice will be taken remains to be seen. Middle-class missions and denominations might prove to be slow in changing their status quo. They might continue to feel that carpeted floors, suits and ties, Charles Wesley's hymns, grammatical Spanish, three-point alliterated sermons, dignified worship, and pipe organs are values worth preserving whether or not they appeal to the Latin American proletariat. They might feel altogether too uncomfortable with people who bathe only infrequently, have holes in their shoes, spit on the floor, clap when they sing, need a handout now and then, and sleep the whole family in a single bedroom. If so, their mediocre growth pattern will probably continue.

Pentecostals do not feel these inhibitions, and therefore will probably continue to grow among the lower classes. They also avoid another inhibition that is characteristic of other groups: they are not particularly concerned with debating the pros and cons of so-called proselytism.

Most Protestants in Latin America are converted Catholics. With the current changes taking place within Catholicism as a result of the Second Vatican Council, many Latin American Protestants are now questioning whether evangelists should continue to encourage Catholics to leave their church. Some suggest that, instead, Catholics who are converted should stay within their church and try to influence it from within. There is undoubtedly some merit to this point of view, but it is not our purpose to settle that thorny question here. The point we are making is that Pentecostals in Latin America will undoubtedly continue for many years to come to bring Catholics not only to a personal faith in Christ, but also to Pentecostal churches.

Not only have they avoided the inhibition of converting Catholics, but Pentecostals also refuse to be inhibited by institutional comity. Comity means simply to respect the territory of other Protestant churches and not to move into their area and compete with them. Non-Pentecostals, in Norbert Johnson's opinion, "have become unduly squeamish about proselytizing." [9]

In this sense, Pentecostals have been successful in keeping the perspective of the lost world before them. If ninety percent of the people of a given village, district, city, or neighborhood were Christians, soundly converted and active in their churches, comity would then be an important principle. But when the churches have discipled only five or ten percent, and where ninety percent have yet to believe, comity becomes rather ludicrous. The Bible says to pray that the Lord send more, not fewer, laborers into the harvest field (Mt. 9:37-38). When the harvest is safely in the barn, the laborers can rest, but not before. Pentecostals in general have no intention of resting, even if they anticipate that they will be accused of sheep-stealing and violation of comity. Reaching lost souls consistently takes a higher priority with them.

The "fertile soil" principle applies equally as well to another biblical analogy. Jesus made His disciples "catchers of men." (Lk. 5:10) We are to win souls like fishermen catch fish. But suppose a fisherman gets into his boat on the shore of the lake, looks out over the water, and sees a cluster of boats toward the horizon. He will not say, "Oh, I will respect those men who are pulling in the fish over there, and go somewhere else to see if I can find some other fish that are biting." No, unless he is unusual, he will row over and fish where the fish are known to be biting. Few will criticize him for that sound fisherman's strategy.

Neither should Pentecostals be unduly criticized for apparent violations of comity, when their vision is on the lost world. It is true that in some cases they have intentionally tried to snatch fish from their neighbor's boat, and when that occurs they deserve to be reprimanded. But my impression is that such cases have been relatively few. Pentecostal growth cannot be explained by Protestants who have transferred church membership. Those millions of first generation Pentecostal Christians in Latin America have for the most part come from the world.

Pentecostals know how to sow in fertile soil. They send laborers into ripe harvest fields. Experienced fishermen go where the fish are biting. The results speak for themselves.

6

Body Life Builds Healthy Churches

When just about every member of the church is active in some ministry or other, the church is bound to grow. To most Pentecostals in Latin America, being a Christian means, among other things, working for God. In contrast to more lethargic churches where the pastor and perhaps a deacon or two are virtually the only active workers in the church, Pentecostal pastors often find themselves cast in the enviable role of coaches of the team. They provide the leadership and the organization, but most of the work out on the streets and in the homes is done by the troops.

While visiting Santiago, Chile, I was once invited by Javier Vásquez, pastor of the Jotabeche Methodist Pentecostal Church, to give a Bible study to a group of men on Tuesday night.

Vásquez referred to them as the "volunteer corps." I was glad to accept the invitation, but I became discouraged when a torrential rainstorm blackened the city late that afternoon. As the meeting time approached it seemed to become worse and worse with spectacular displays of thunder and lightning. By the time I got on and off the bus my shoes were filled with water, and my spirits were as drenched as my clothes. I wondered why I went through with it, for surely no one would come to Bible study.

Pastor Vásquez actually did apologize to me for the poor attendance that night. Because of the weather, only about 400 men had come out! The usual attendance, he explained, was at least double that amount. Later on I was amazed to discover that these men had not come out to church only for a Bible study—they had come to receive their instructions as to what each of them was to do for the rest of the week!

Each one was assigned his duties according to the gifts of the Spirit he had. The volunteer corps was organized like a mini-army with a clear administrative chain of command so that all were directly accountable to an appointed leader. Some were sent to minister in jails, some visited hospitals, some called on church members who were having a problem of one kind or another, some preached in open air meetings, some concentrated their efforts on starting a new congregation, some prayed for the sick, some surveyed a new area to discover whether the people there were responsive to the gospel.

All 400 of them were, in the truest biblical sense of the word, "ministers," actively doing their thing for the Lord. If the paid pastors were the only "ministers," Pentecostal churches could not grow as they do. But when all members of the body function together as they should, wonderful things happen.

The idea of all members of the body working together has recently been called "body life." The term did not originate either in Latin America or in a Pentecostal church. It comes from Pastor Ray Stedman of the Peninsula Bible Church in Palo Alto, California. Stedman has popularized the phrase in a book by the same title,[1] but the concept is still relatively new to many Christians. Not to Latin American Pentecostals, however, because they have been practicing body life for decades, even though they might not use the term as such.

"Body life" describes in a succinct way what 1 Corinthians 12 teaches. The church is compared to a body there—the body of Christ. Christ is the head, and all Christians are members. Every member of the body, when he becomes a Christian, is placed in his position by the Holy Spirit, and he is expected to function there. In othe words, each one is given a spiritual gift. No Christian is allowed to choose his own gift; it is assigned by the Holy Spirit. The Christian's responsibility is to discover just what his gift is, and then use it for the benefit of the body as a whole.

One of the tragedies of contemporary Christianity is that so many church members have not yet discovered their spiritual gifts, and therefore are not using them. Some don't even realize they have one, simply because no one has ever adequately taught them 1 Corinthians 12 or Romans 12. They are, therefore, not able to please the

Lord as they should. They are like the timid man in the parable of the talents (Mt. 25:14-30) who buried his talent when he should have been using it. When he met his Lord, he was labeled a "wicked, lazy slave." (Mt. 25:26) If, somehow, we could dig up and put into use all the buried talents in our Christian churches, I am convinced we would release enough latent spiritual power to win the world for Christ.

While it must be admitted that not every single Pentecostal in Latin America is doing his part, there is no question that the percentage of those who are is higher in Pentecostal churches than in the slower growing churches. The gift of evangelism is particularly prominent there. Furthermore, every believer is instructed to be an aggressive witness, whether he has the gift of evangelism or not. The real spiritual hero is the soul winner, the fisher of men. The Holy Spirit gives power to persuade men and women to follow Christ in repentance, faith, and baptism, and all Christians are expected to use that power.

The United Pentecostal Church in Pereira, Colombia, for example, has three skilled evangelistic teams organized in its congregation of 310. Each team has fifteen members who visit and witness constantly according to well-planned strategy. Often on a Sunday a group of men and women will hire a number of taxis to take them to a neighboring village. They spend the whole day in visitation, saturating the community with the gospel, and inviting the responsive people to an evangelistic service in the evening.

When a group of believers is gathered there, the new town becomes a "preaching point" and is assigned to a different team for continuing evangelization. The objective is to win new people to Christ and organize a new church as soon as possible.

In a period of two years the Pereira church had established twenty-one preaching points with regular attendance of more than 350, already more than doubling their own church membership.[2]

Methods of effective evangelism differ from place to place. Pentecostals have not succumbed to the danger of institutionalizing a particular evangelistic program. They have not attempted to "package" what may have succeeded in one country and ship it out far and wide, like an exported commodity. The Methodist Pentecostals in Santiago reap abundantly through street preaching, and the Brazil for Christ Church attributes much of its evangelistic fruit to a widespread radio ministry. The *Congregacao Crista* in Brazil knows what others are doing, but they have rejected both street preaching and radio in favor of the individual, person-to-person witness of each member.

The *Congregacao Crista* believes so much in body life that they refuse to hire pastors for their churches. They believe that the Holy Spirit provides each church with all the gifts needed for healthy church life, and that when members are properly using their gifts, a professional minister is simply excess baggage. The elders and the deacons do the preaching. The only man the church hires is the bookkeeper; the rest of the work is done by the members themselves.[3]

This is exceedingly effective. The Sao Paulo traffic police are accustomed to regular traffic jams in the Brás area when the *Congregacao Crista* meets on Wednesday and Sunday nights, packing their 7,000-seat auditorium. More traditional churches, where professional, seminary-trained pastors are hired seem to have no traffic problems. In the city of Sao Paulo, for example, the older Presbyterian church counts only 8,000 members in contrast to the 110,000 of the *Congregacao Crista*.

The point is, that regardless of the method of evangelism used, Pentecostal churches have effectively mobilized their members. Notice that not every Pentecostal is equally effective as an evangelist, although every one is a witness. The whole body is not an eye; if it were, how could it hear (1 Co. 12:17)? The principle of body life is not that everyone does the same thing, but that everyone does something, according to the gifts the Spirit of God has given him.

But whatever any member does, it is geared toward the singular goal of effective evangelism. Not every player on a football team scores points, but everyone plays hard toward that end. Quarterbacks on winning teams make the headlines, but they wouldn't if it weren't for the guards and tackles. Likewise, soul winners make the Pentecostal "headlines," but their effectiveness in frontline evangelism is due to a large extent to the fact that the whole body is healthy and functioning well.

Part of the action of the body involves instructing new believers. When church growth is rapid with the Lord adding to the church daily such as should be saved, properly caring for the new believers is altogether impossible if the body life principle is not in effect. More traditional churches, which expect their hired pastoral staffs to take care of the "follow up," have a built-in factor which retards growth. There is no way they can grow adequately, because of a pure and simple lack of manpower.

As we have mentioned previously, the Great Commission not only commands believers to "go" and "make disciples," but also to "baptize" and "teach." Donald McGavran has rephrased these four steps in bucolic terms: seeking, finding, folding, and feeding.[4] Evangelism which stops short at either seeking or finding will not result in church growth. The lost sheep must be brought into the fold and properly fed. In churches where conversions and baptisms are counted by the tens and twenties, this is not a problem for a paid staff to handle. And when they move up into the hundreds and thousands, even more help is needed. Every member of the body needs to do his part.

In Colombia, for example, when a person is converted through a member of the Assemblies of God, he at once becomes the center of much attention. His new brethren in Christ will surround him with love and concern, making sure he begins to attend church regularly. Within a week he is encouraged to join an indoctrination class. His faith is not allowed to cool. The new lamb is folded and fed. He at once begins to study a special booklet, used all through the denomination, designed to prepare him for baptism and church membership. Right from the beginning, he is taught not only about the Church and the Christian life, but he also is introduced to the evangelistic goals of the Assemblies of God. He is taught to be an

— 83 —

active member of the team, a functioning part of the body.[5]

When the body life principle is in action, and every Christian is in the biblical sense of the word a "minister," one would expect that the differences between clergy and laity would diminish. This is largely true in Latin American Pentecostal churches. It does not mean that paid pastors are rejected by all groups the way they are in the *Congregacao Crista* and some others. The majority of Pentecostal churches have paid pastors, but this is an application, rather than an extension, of the body life principle. Generally speaking, Pentecostal pastors have become pastors because of the way that God has previously enabled them to function in the body.

Almost invariably, before they became recognized as pastors and hired by the churches, they spent years working as unpaid laymen. This is in contrast to the more traditional systems such as the Catholic church which puts young boys in a convent and raises them as priests, or many Protestant churches which choose promising young men (older boys in this case) and send them through a professional training school such as a Bible institute or seminary *before* they have functioned as active, adult members of the body for a significant time.

Just how this is done will be described in the next chapter, but here it is important to stress that because of the body life principle the Pentecostals in Latin America have not fallen into an exaggerated professionalization of the clergy as more static churches have done. Pentecostal ministers are really laymen, and Pentecostal laymen are ministers. It should be no surprise that God is blessing this system. A fresh examination of the pastoral epistles will show that it applies some valuable biblical principles.

Up to this point not much has been said about Pentecostal missionaries to Latin America. One of the reasons is that Pentecostal churches are not typically missionary-dominated churches as are many of the others. The statistics in *Latin American Church Growth*, for example, show that the non-Pentecostals (faith missions, newer denominations, Adventists, and traditional denominations) have ninety percent of the missionaries but only thirty-seven percent of the members, while the Pentecostals have ten percent of the missionaries with a whopping sixty-three percent of the members.[6]

Some of the reasons for this, such as the ability of Pentecostal missionaries to identify with the responsive proletariat, have already been mentioned. But in this section on spiritual gifts, another quality of Pentecostal missionaries must be stressed. This is their emphasis on the evangelistic and church-planting function of missionaries. One of the clearest expressions of this emphasis has been made by Melvin Hodges, who for many years has been the Latin American Secretary for the Assemblies of God in the United States, and thus the leader of one of the largest bodies of Pentecostal missionaries in Latin America. Hodges says this:

> In pioneering a new area, the missionary exercises his first and most important ministry as a planter of churches. Here the missionary must be evangelist to the unconverted and teacher of the newborn con-

verts. Instead of settling down to pastor the first group of converts that he raises up, the missionary should remain mobile and keep the vision for the entire district.[7]

A mission society which considers the "first and most important ministry" of its missionaries as the planting of churches is starting right off in a growth situation. Missionaries are recruited in the homeland, not so much on their ability to lead choirs, teach mathematics, organize labor unions, exegete the Greek New Testament, increase egg production, refute Rudolph Bultmann, or coach volleyball teams—good as each one of those qualities might be. Pentecostal missions are not organized so much to serve the church in Latin America as to win those not yet in the church to Christ, and bring them into the body.

Churches in Latin America, as in other parts of the world, function surprisingly well under the leadership of national believers, gifted by the Holy Spirit, and moving forward by body life. Pentecostal missionaries know that such well-intentioned activities as so-called "institutional missions," "service missions," or "interchurch aid" have their place, but that they have not always been effective in winning the world. Too often they have resulted in a kind of subtle paternalism which has retarded, rather than accelerated, church growth.

Missions, in the best tradition, do not flow from one church to another church, but rather from a church to the world. This is what Hodges means by "keeping the vision." Recent missionary history has shown us that much too often our missionary societies, both liberal and evangelical, have lost the vision of the world and fallen into what I have called elsewhere the "syndrome of church development." [8] The official policy statement of the Foreign Missions Department of the Assemblies of God assiduously avoids this sort of a paternalistic trend, as well as the other extreme which can be equally dangerous.

It reads, under the subheading, "Missionary Objectives:"

> The missionary must not abdicate his responsibility to world evangelism and church planting, either by perpetuating the mission's authority over the national church or by *succumbing to nationalistic interests* that would prevent him from fulfilling the Great Commission.[9]

The italics on the phrase "succumbing to nationalistic interests" are mine, since I feel this should be stressed. Many missionary societies feel more inhibited at this point than Pentecostals seem to. Some missionary societies, because of nationalistic pressures from members of their own churches in foreign countries, have recalled their missionaries and offered them pastorates in the homeland.

While it is true that in some cases political considerations have made this necessary, I am afraid that the more frequent cause has been a hypersensitivity to the kind of ecclesiastical nationalism that has unfortunately dimmed the vision of the world. Although it may be painful to do so, there are times when the mission must be courageous enough to fulfill the Great Commission out there in the world whether the national church wants it to or not.

Pentecostal churches are growing so rapidly

that there is a continually high ratio between nationals and missionaries, thus reducing tendencies toward paternalism on one side and misguided nationalism on the other. This is a healthy pattern in which all Christians, both missionaries and nationals, have the liberty to function as members of the body according to their spiritual gifts. It is a practical application of body life.

7

Seminaries in the Streets

Several times now we have mentioned the Jotabeche Methodist Pentecostal Church of Santiago, Chile. One of the offspring of the revival under Hoover in 1909, this church has developed into a microcosm of much of Latin American Pentecostalism. It is not the largest church, but its 16,000-seat sanctuary is impressive. It may not even be the purest church; its members may not be the most active, or its worship service may not be the most uplifting. But if none of these is true, the Jotabeche Church will not be far down on any of the lists. All in all, it is one of the truly typical Pentecostal churches on the continent.

The reason for stressing this is to introduce the pastor of the Jotabeche Church, Rev. Javier

Vásquez. Vásquez is a mature man, probably finishing his fifties, of medium build, with straight black hair and a strong, square jaw. His movements, like his words, are slow and deliberate. His air is serious, although he has a ready smile. He dresses in a dark suit, white shirt, and dark tie with little concern for style or tailoring. If he changed his clothes and put on a blue cap, he would look every bit like a railroad engineer. His whole appearance and manner identify him with the common people who make up his congregation.

Although he is little known outside of Chile, Javier Vásquez is without doubt one of the most significant churchmen in Christendom. I have not been able to confirm this to my entire satisfaction, but information from reliable sources claims that when Vásquez was elected pastor of the Jotabeche Church, he received 40,000 secret-ballot votes. These would have come not only from members of the mother church, but from her multiple daughter churches scattered all over the capital city. Even so, few pastors I can think of in the United States could claim even ten percent of that number of votes behind his pastoral call.

To provide the leadership for such an enormous church. Vásquez needs well-seasoned pastoral and administrative gifts. On the platform, he needs the charisma to handle the huge crowd, allowing them the proper measure of freedom of expression balanced with the discipline which will keep them attentive during the sermon. He does his job well, and is loved by his people.

I have no details as to Vásquez' financial condition. By all outward appearances, he is a humble man who lives unostentatiously. Undoubtedly, however, he is taken care of adequately. David Brackenridge gives a notable description of the typical Pentecostal pastor:

> It is astonishing to note the care and reverence the people show towards their pastor. Everything is done for him. Besides monetary support, members bring gifts of meat, vegetables, and fruit. His table is usually full. He entertains lavishly, and no member is turned away who is in need. But it must be said that the pastor controls everything—finances and all the activities. Nothing is done without his consent.[1]

How are men like Javier Vásquez trained? Where do they learn to preach and carry such heavy pastoral responsiblity? Uninitiated visitors have asked Vásquez where he went to seminary. He answers without hesitation, "Out there in the streets. I would want no other."

Is this sour grapes? Not for Vásquez. He is well known abroad enough to have been offered lavish study scholarships. He undoubtedly could pick his institution if he wanted to take further study almost any place in the world. But although he might not articulate it with any great fluency, intuitively he knows that more important than all the academic honors and degrees in Europe or the United States is maintaining identification with the people God has called him to minister to.

It is not that Vásquez has never seen churches which insist on seminary-trained pastors. Santiago has scores of them, and Vásquez rubs shoulders with the ministers. While he is humble enough to admit that he needs to know more Bible and theology, he is realistic enough to see that seminary training has its negative, as well as positive, effects there in his Latin American context. Vásquez notices that many of the churches with highly trained pastors are meeting the needs of only a very few people; they continually struggle with program after program to keep "relevant"; their services are dull and uninviting; their budgets show an excessive amount of red ink, and their evangelistic impact is minimal.

Even though their pastors make close friends with government officials, enjoy expense-paid jaunts abroad to important international conferences, debate theology and social ethics on high levels, speak English fluently, and publish scholarly articles in ecclesiastical journals, Pentecostal pastors like Vásquez do not feel in the least envious. Nor do they spend much time criticizing the others. They just keep on with what they know is God's calling for them—bringing multitudes of Chileans to repentance and faith in Jesus Christ.

While Pentecostal pastors might not be able to discuss the history and philosophy of theological education on a level with men like Ralph Winter and Ted Ward, they do raise similar questions. For one thing, they ask whether the slow growth of non-Pentecostal churches might in fact have something to do with the way their ministers are trained. They tend to think it might, and therefore they are not generally anxious to change. Many outsiders have offered to "help" them with funds, personnel, and know-how. Such groups as the World Council of Churches, some faith missions, newer denominations, and others would set up a seminary program for them at the drop of a hat, but the Pentecostals are not ready to drop the hat.

A recent study of the Protestant clergy in Chile has brought some remarkable facts to the surface.[2] Non-Pentecostal pastors are divided fifty-fifty according to age: half are over forty and half are under forty. But a full eighty-two percent of Pentecostal pastors are over forty years of age. In the category of under thirty, the non-Pentecostals have twenty-three percent of their pastors, while Pentecostals have only three percent. In other words, Pentecostal pastors are for the most part older, experienced men.

Even more revealing, perhaps, is the comparison of educational levels. No non-Pentecostal pastors of those surveyed had less than full primary education. But fifty-six percent of the Pentecostal pastors had not finished primary school. Apparently, then, academic achievement is not considered by Pentecostals in Latin America as an important qualification for the ministry.

One other aspect of the survey will help our understanding of Pentecostal ministers. Of the non-Pentecostal pastors, seventy-eight percent were second generation Protestants, while Pentecostals reverse the ratio with seventy-nine percent first generation, converted from the world, Christians. Think of what this means. We see here what is most likely a demonstration of McGavran's theory of "redemption and lift."[3] Christian redemption so cleans up the personal life and so changes human values, that often it will lift a family from a lower social class to the middle class. This is good, as long as the lifted family does not lose their contact with the masses, and disqualify themselves from winning their friends and relatives to Christ.

Redeemed people, generally speaking, adopt

new educational values. They say, "I want my children to have the advantages I missed." They encourage their children to go through secondary school and a university. In other words, they want their children to have a middle-class education, marry a middle-class girl, and live in a middle-class neighborhood. There is nothing wrong with this, and one could hardly wish anything else for brethren in Christ.

But whenever this happens, one should not be surprised that the *evangelistic effectiveness* of this second generation man is drastically reduced. To pick up the terminology from chapter five, he has moved from fertile soil (the masses) to relatively barren soil (the classes). Among other things, he has also virtually disqualified himself from being a grass-roots Pentecostal pastor.

The study we have been referring to confirms this theory of redemption and lift.[4] It shows that there is virtually no difference between the social class origins of Pentecostal and non-Pentecostal pastors. About seventy percent of all pastors were born into lower-class homes. But because most non-Pentecostal pastors were raised in Christian homes, they were converted as young people. They then had more educational advantages, and they tended to lose contact with the fertile field of the lower class where they were born. Pentecostal pastors, on the other hand, were converted as adults and never made a radical break from their social contacts.

With this profile of Pentecostal pastors, we can better understand both how they are trained and how this training helps Pentecostal churches to grow. Some outsiders, when they first hear about them, feel sorry for Pentecostal pastors and their "seminaries in the streets." But further examination reveals that this is in all probability a surprisingly high quality of training for the pastorate. As a matter of fact, it may well be that people from the outside who, with a generous heart, advocate reform in this area, might unwittingly be cutting away at one of the tap roots of Latin American Pentecostalism. It would be a shame if the desire for more educational respectability in the Pentecostal ministry eventually brought Pentecostal church growth to a grinding halt.

Candidates for the Pentecostal street seminaries look much more like the description of Christian leaders in 1 Timothy than the average student in a traditional seminary. Since they are older, they can be judged as candidates for the pastorate, not on what they *might be* when they get older, but on what they have *proven to be*. They have a wife and a family that they govern well, they are not novices, they are patient, sober-minded, and temperate. Moreover, they have a good report by them which are outside the fellowship, something that younger persons who have not yet made an adult contribution to society can hardly claim.

These Christian men who have been gifted by God for the pastorate are not sent far away to some institution for three years or so. They stay with their families, they work at their jobs, they keep their social contacts, they worship with their people, and with all this they learn by doing. They learn their skills like craftsmen through the ages have learned—by apprenticeship. They feel that the best place to learn how to be a pastor is with pastor and people, not so much with theologians and scholars.

The apprenticeship system actually makes becoming a pastor a more difficult procedure than a traditional seminary education. Success in the ministry itself becomes the qualifying factor, not the awarding of a diploma or a degree. The final exam is confirmation through actual experience that God has given the appropriate gifts, and that the man, through the power of the Holy Spirit, knows how to exercise them effectively.

There is no stereotyped system that all Pentecostal churches in Latin America follow for training their pastors. Almost all of them, however, involve apprenticeship in one way or another. When a man becomes pastor, he typically has had an abundance of previous experience in all aspects of church work, but different Pentecostal churches use different titles for their hierarchy. Here is one of the typical ladders which leads up to the status of pastor in a Pentecostal church: [5]

1. *Street preacher.* As we pointed out in chapter three, almost every convert is expected to be a witness for Christ, and in some cases he must go out in the street the following Sunday to give his testimony in public. This means that every believer is a candidate for this first rung of the ladder, and therefore each one has some possibility of the pastorate before him. Experience will soon reveal which of the believers who give their testimonies in the streets have the pastoral gifts, and the successful ones may move up to the next rung.

2. *Sunday School teacher.* Some Pentecostal churches have Sunday School, some don't. But all have Bible classes of one kind or another, and those who show up well in the streets are invited to take a class. If the teacher finds he

can communicate simple Bible truths to his students, and hold the interest of his class, he passes this test and goes up another rung.

3. *"Preacher."* When the pastor asks one of his men to be a "preacher," this means that he will be permitted to lead worship services, and occasionally take the sermon in smaller meetings. If the apprentice shows ability in this ministry and his pastor is pleased with his performance, he qualifies for the next rung.

4. *New preaching point.* When he is sent out by the pastor to a new preaching point, he carries a heavier responsibility. He must evangelize an assigned area, and his success there is measured by nothing less than converts. If, through his ministry, men and women are coming to faith in Christ and transformed lives are evident, this is interpreted as the will of God that the man obtain official recognition by the denomination. The next rung up is his first official position.

5. *Christian worker.* In order to become an official Christian worker, the pastor must present the candidate's name to the Annual Conference with his recommendation. This step is taken seriously, and by no means do all those who enter the apprentice system of training make it this far. Many remain in the ranks, doing their best for the Lord. As a Christian worker, the man comes under the denominational leadership, and wider ministries open to him outside the sphere of influence of his local church.

6. *Pastor-deacon.* If he is promoted to pastor-deacon, he is usually assigned a new area of the city or a village where he is expected to plant a new church. In fact, planting a new church

is a requirement for confirmation on this rung of the ladder. If he cannot do this successfully, he rises no further, and does not make the category of pastor, the final rung.

7. *Pastor.* The Annual Conference will take the action of naming the probationer to full pastor only when he is tested and found true. Here the test involves economics. Not only must he plant a church, but he must nurture it until it becomes large and solvent enough to support him financially as pastor. When the pastor can present sufficient evidence that he can leave his secular employment to dedicate himself entirely to the pastorate, he will be awarded the title.

There is no set time for the trip up the ladder. A young person might spend fifteen or twenty years at it until his maturity and leadership ability have been accepted by the churches. This apprenticeship system sifts and sorts until men who fit biblical patterns of leadership emerge. It does not pass older men by as do some traditional theological training institutions. One man was converted at the age of fifty-eight in a Pentecostal church in Nicaragua. He was gifted for the pastorate, and the Assemblies of God there had a training program which he entered at age sixty. For the next fifteen years he served effectively as pastor of a Nicaraguan church.[6]

Where Pentecostals do have the more traditional type of Bible institutes, they often are characterized by a flexibility that builds in the type of training we have described. Theoretical training, or knowledge for its own sake have no place there. All training is functional, geared for effectiveness in the ministry.

One Pentecostal Bible institute in Central America has been highly productive as a center for evangelism and church planting for many years. Its requirements for graduation are unusual, but effective in extending the Kingdom of God. The institute admits a first-year student even if he has little or no experience in the ministry, but when that year is over, he is sent to a new field to plant a church. He can only be readmitted for further studies after he has successfully planted a church, which in turn is able to support him in his continuing education. By that time, he has become an experienced worker and is much more highly motivated to learn.

Most pastors trained by the apprenticeship system would like to learn more, but they feel the price for that learning is too high if it means enrollment in a traditional Bible institute or seminary. The burgeoning movement of theological education by extension throughout Latin America is a welcome addition as far as thousands of Pentecostal pastors are concerned. They now can have their cake and eat it too. Through extension, the full curriculum of a seminary can be taught to them right there in their churches. Quality of training is improved all the way around because the same material is taught, not to youngsters in a secluded institution, but to mature leaders out there on the front lines. The theological education by extension movement has succeeded in taking theological training out of the ivory towers and onto the streets—right where the Pentecostals had it in the first place.

A great deal could be written about this, but it is amply covered in readily available sources and need not be repeated.[7] It is hoped that at least in this area of churchmanship, the non-Pentecostals will look very carefully at the successful Pentecostal patterns of "seminaries in the streets" and learn some much-needed lessons. One result might well be the beginning of accelerated church growth in churches which now are barely holding their own.

8
It's Fun To Go To Church

The top leader of the ecumenical movement in Latin America is Uruguayan Methodist
Emilio Castro. From his vantage point as the head
of UNELAM, the counterpart of the World Council
of Churches,* he can often see significant trends.
In a recent report, Castro, no Pentecostal himself,
makes the following statement which has important implications for discovering the secrets of
Pentecostal growth:

It is safe to say that Pentecostalism is probably
the most "indigenous" Latin American kind of Prot-

---

* Since writing this, Castro has been promoted to the
position of Director of the Commission on World Mission
and Evangelism of the World Council of Churches and
has moved to Geneva.

estantism. . . . Because they are not institutionally bound to churches in other parts of the world—and consequently are not economically dependent on foreign groups—Pentecostal churches may be said to represent authentic Latin American Protestantism.[1]

The remarkable way that Pentecostal churches have been able to take on the shape of the culture in which they are growing gives Pentecostals an appeal that other churches seem to attain only with great difficulty. Generally speaking, Pentecostals have become more indigenous to Latin America than liberals on one hand and fundamentalists on the other. Foreign influence and control have been minimal in the development of Latin American Pentecostalism. While it is true that missionaries were involved in planting the Pentecostal churches at first, the subsequent growth of the churches was in many cases so rapid that the foreigners could not have controlled the national churches even if they had wanted to.

Missionary paternalism is much more likely to occur in situations of slow growth. Ten missionary couples can have an overbearing influence on a church of 100 members, and this in influence will be felt no matter how hard the missionaries try to avoid it. But when the ten couples are working alongside a church of 100,000, it is a different story. In a large, growing church, even a "great White Father" type of missionary can rarely succeed in dominating the church.

In Chile, Willis Hoover exercised considerable influence over the Methodist Pentecostal Church while he was alive. But happily he did not build a missionary empire. He did not recruit other foreigners to take his place. He did not feel that the nationals were incapable of leading the church "Since Hoover's time," J.B.A. Kessler says, "no more foreigners have been connected with the indigenous Pentecostal movement, and all negative nationalism has of itself come to an end."[2]

Many non-Pentecostal missions have been much slower to turn over new churches to national leaders. This lingering paternalism almost invariably produces two results which retard church growth. The first is a foreignness about the church so that it appears to be something both exotic and irrelevant to outsiders. The second is the development of a strong anti-missionary sentiment, particularly in second generation believers.

Results of lingering Paternalism

The syndrome of church development creeps up so subtly that missions often do not recognize that they should have taken their hands off church affairs long ago. Then when the tensions between missionaries and nationals build up to the breaking point, the turnover becomes a traumatic experience with the outbreak of severe nationalism, wounded personal feelings on both sides, and consequent slow growth. Human energies, both missionary and national, are dissipated on internal troubleshooting rather than on winning the world to Christ.

The ability of Pentecostal missions willingly to turn God's work over to nationals might possibly be traced to their strong emphasis on the Holy Spirit. The Bible promises that the Holy Spirit will guide believers of all nationalities into all truth (Jn. 16:13), and Pentecostal missionaries are more likely to take that literally than others might be. In the final analysis, they do not let their decision as to turning over the work depend so much on whether they can trust their national brethren as to whether they can trust the Holy Spirit. In this area the Pentecostal trust index is high.

Non-Pentecostal missionaries sometimes are unable to recognize that educational standards can insidiously substitute for simple trust in the Holy Spirit. The cliché that "my job is to work myself out of a job" is the cause of some of these problems. The missionary who says this tends to think in terms of a national *replacing a missionary* as over against a national *leading his own church.* There is a tremendous difference between the two, especially for a missionary who belongs to a mission which is proud of "keeping its educational standards high." The missionaries all have had primary and secondary schooling, followed by Bible college and even in some cases seminary. When they go on furlough, the mission almost by reflex action replaces them with an equally well-trained missionary.

The operation of cultural overhang here is obvious. In an effort to exhibit Christian humility, the missionary says to himself, "I wish I could do a better job. I could if I had more training. The training I have had only barely qualifies me for my job." Once he says this, and once he combines it with the compulsion that he has to train nationals to take his job, the missionary is caught in a web. He must see to it that the national at the very least attains his own standards, so he develops a program for primary and secondary school, Bible Institute, and seminary. In some cases the missionary even aspires to send the national leader abroad for the final polish, most frequently to his own country and to his own *alma mater*. When this happens (and if by some miracle the national does not join the "brain drain" in the process), the missionary feels he can turn some of the work over.

Then the surprise comes. The years and years that this process has taken has deeply incrusted missionary paternalism into the church. Educational standards have been imposed which are foreign to the culture of the church members. Institutions have been developed to meet these standards which can only be staffed and financed by missionaries, and these have become an integral part of the church. Academic degrees have unconsciously been elevated above Holy Spirit gifts and power. The syndrome of church development has again run its course. If the missionaries were to pull out completely, it is questionable whether the church could survive. Poor church!

Happily, all non-Pentecostal churches in Latin America are not like the stereotype I have just described. But enough are to make this a widespread problem, and one that honest missionaries will immediately acknowledge. There is little hope that a church like this can become significantly indigenous, at least within the present generation.

Foreign ways of doing things have been deeply associated in the minds of the nationals themselves with spiritual Christianity. Hymns by Fanny Crosby and Isaac Watts, played on pianos and organs, may be considered *more spiritual* than those written by nationals to national musical rhythms and played on guitars and maracas, incredible as that may seem. Music that pleases the ear and makes the foot tap, regardless of how eloquently the lyrics praise God, is considered worldly, not only by missionaries, but also by some nationals!

Church music is a part of what I like to call liturgy. The word liturgy is sometimes closely associated with very ritualistic churches, but it need not be. In its broadest sense, it simply means the form a church has chosen to use to worship God. It is ironic to see some churches which repudiate any liturgy at all actively developing their own non-liturgical liturgy anyway.

What I have been leading up to so far in this chapter is this: largely because Pentecostal churches have been allowed to become indigenous very early in their development, they have developed a culturally-relevant liturgy. This is one important reason why Pentecostal churches are growing in Latin America.

One of the first things you notice when you go into a worship service in a Latin American Pentecostal church is how much the people seem to be enjoying themselves. The hardest thing to find in one of the Pentecostal services is a wide yawn. Unfortunately, yawns are all too common in many other churches in Latin America. Services are boring, and for many it is a chore to go to church once or twice on Sunday, but it is a Christian exercise that must be taken, so the faithful put up with it.

The problem is that while believers might have

enough self-motivation to do their weekly spiritual calisthenics, they are reluctant to invite their unsaved friends and neighbors to participate. They know by experience that their dull liturgy turns off the average Latin American, and consequently evangelism becomes difficult and ineffective.

But since Pentecostals have fun going to church, they do not hesitate to bring others along. They know ahead of time that when they lead another person to Christ, they can bring that newborn babe to a spiritual home he will enjoy. The Pentecostal community is Latin American enough in every way to make Latin Americans feel at home. Culturally-relevant liturgy thus becomes a strong growth factor.

What does Latin American Pentecostal liturgy look like? In order to answer this question, I have classified the most important elements under eight headings:

1. *The bigness.* Size in itself can produce very beneficial psychological results. This is the "rally" aspect of church life. Bigness is at times threatening because bigness can work against another equally important aspect of church life—the community. If, along with bigness, the church does not provide structures through which Christians can form intimate relationships with each other, where they can hurt together and bleed together and rejoice together and encourage one another on the gut level, then size itself is worthless. But the community aspect of Latin American Pentecostalism is described in other chapters. Here our attention is on what Pentecostals do when they all come together to worship.

When unbelievers walk into the Portales Church

in Mexico City or the Brazil for Christ Church in Sao Paulo or the Hidalgo Church in Buenos Aires or the Jotabeche Church in Santiago, they know they are in the midst of something highly unusual. Literally thousands of people gathering together weekly at the same time in the same place, not for a soccer game or a bull fight or a political demonstration, but to worship God, is an attractive spectacle. In a real sense it is an effective evangelistic tool.

But not only is it appealing to unbelievers, it helps build up the believers and strengthen their faith. Believers feel like they are winners. They develop positive thinking, and benefit from the power that accompanies it. They are encouraged when they know they are part of something big. When they go out into the world, they go with a self-confidence and optimism that radiates to others and makes them more effective in their witness than they might otherwise be.

One observer has described the effect of the bigness of the Brazil for Christ Church in Sao Paulo in these graphic terms:

> Packing into the public buses, perhaps singing as they come, they converge on their temple. From all parts of the city and outlying areas they come, ready to share the joy and excitement of a great throng of believers on the Saturday night. They pray, sing, witness, and hear their leader. Tomorrow they will be scattered in hundreds of congregations around the city, many of which are small and struggling. But they will not be discouraged: they know they are part of a *people*, a *movement*! Something is happening, something big, something God-sized. They have seen it and felt it.[3]

Bigness helps generate the power to produce more bigness.

2. *The social opportunity.* Believers in the Pentecostal churches are not anonymous. They relate to each other well. Many arrive a full half hour before the service starts in order to see their friends, exchange warm *abrazos*, inquire about the health of their families, and share experiences. This social free-for-all is more reminiscent of a railroad station than Westminster Cathedral, but it makes sense to Latin Americans who by nature are much more personable and emotional than Anglo-Saxons.

Latin American churches that suffer from the cultural overhang of their Anglo-Saxon founders are somber by contrast. They have been taught that in that period before church begins "the Lord is in His holy temple; let all the earth keep silence before Him." A time of social intercourse in the sanctuary seems to them to be unspiritual and a violation of true worship. They insist that you come to church to talk to God, not to each other.

3. *The noise level.* Christians who feel this way about church also tend to feel that when you talk to God you should do so quietly. Prayer is most typically either led by the minister in a well-modulated voice, or a "time of silent prayer." In other words, the noise level in the average church is very similar to any church you would find in Scotland or Saxony or South Dakota. A baby's whimper becomes a major distraction.

Pentecostals in Latin America don't feel this about church, however. Even in times of prayer, the noise level is high. Simultaneous prayer is common practice. When it comes time for talking to God, everybody in the room talks to Him, and the noise rises to a loud roar. The exuberant worshipers do not feel particularly inhibited about their own voice levels either, and some actually shout while they are praying.

Is this unspiritual? Hardly. Hundreds of people addressing God together must be some sort of a highly spiritual exercise. Does it aid worship? Yes. It has many beneficial effects on the type of people who are doing it. It produces a sense of high drama, it nourishes the emotions, and it makes the presence of God more real to them. Anthropologist Eugene Nida has observed that this even *helps* people to pray, since it brings prayer from the semi-professional level found in many churches to the level of the common person.

Everybody is invited to pray, and "the contagion is such that one can scarcely avoid praying." [4] Many who would never dare to pray when everyone else was listening lose their timidity and gladly pray when everyone else is doing the same. Mistakes in grammar or lack of ecclesiastical polish are not even noticed by the person in the next seat. To God, they are not important at all.

4. *The participation.* Hardly anybody keeps track of how many persons might actually participate in a typical Pentecostal service, but one researcher took the trouble to count them at a service in Colombia, and came up with a total of sixty-five participants. He speculates that "if missionaries would have had their hand in this, it is unlikely the service would have followed the course it did." [5] It is highly unlikely, because that is not the way Anglo-Saxons usually do things.

For one thing, the high quality professional training and subsequent gulf between clergy and laity that many Anglo-Saxon churches have been living with for generations have tended to cast all responsibility for leading worship on one person, the pastor. Some churches have even had to develop a "Laymen's Sunday" in a pathetic attempt to remedy the situation.

Pentecostal worshipers who do not participate in a direct way participate indirectly, but nevertheless actively. Worship is not a passive experience. It is people-centered rather than platform-centered. The audience participates with "Amen" and "Hallelujah" and "Praise the Lord." The Chilean Pentecostals are well-known for their three-fold "Glory to God." Several times during the average service the opportunity will come for the audience to spring to its feet, throw its arms up into the air, and shout with full volume, "*Gloria a Dios*" three times. The total dramatic effect is breathtaking. To be honest, it's fun!

5. *The motion.* One thing that reduces yawns in Pentecostal churches is the need to keep moving. Worshipers stand up and sit down so frequently that no one settles back enough to get sleepy. Lifting hands up and down also keeps the pulse beating.

In Chile the Methodist Pentecostals have even designed a unique kind of pew to allow for another motion—kneeling to pray. Crowded conditions push the pews so close together that there would not be room enough to kneel, if it weren't for the movable backs on the benches. When the signal is given, the congregation kneels, and everyone pushes on the back of the bench ahead of him. It is so hinged that it moves forward and provides a space for your elbows while you pray. You have to move fast in order not to get slapped across the back by your own bench. The resulting clackity-clack of hundreds of pew backs contributes to the noise level, and thus to the drama of the service.

To increase motion, some of the Pentecostal churches do not send ushers up and down the aisles with offering plates, but rather invite the givers to come forward and lay their offerings on the altar up in the front of the church. While they are doing it the choir might be singing a special number, or the audience might be singing. At first it looks like a violation of the "decently and in order" clause of Paul's instructions to the Corinthians (1 Co. 14:40), but it isn't. It is a carefully-planned and well-disciplined aspect of the Pentecostal liturgical pattern. It is part of the very decency and order that is most relevant to them.

Spiritual dancing introduces a kind of motion into the worship services that the newcomer considers unusual at first, but later finds to be quite enchanting. Ordinarily during congregational singing or during a choir number, several individuals will begin dancing right in their pews, moving their arms and bodies with varying degrees of gracefulness. Some will find their way to the aisles or to open spaces at the back or front of the church. I once saw what must be the most unusual sign ever posted on the wall of a church: "dancing on the stairs prohibited." This was just another indication that not only order, but also physical safety is a concern of Pentecostal brethren.

6. *Tongues.* Speaking in tongues is so common-place in Pentecostal services in Latin America that some of them might wonder why it is listed here as a separate item. Most speaking in tongues occurs during prayer times, so it might more naturally be included as an item under prayer. But since this is being written for non-Pentecostals as well as for Pentecostals, one or two things need to be said about this.

For many members of the proletariat in Latin America, life can easily become a dull, color-less routine. With little excess money to spend on household conveniences, automobiles, vacations, or entertainment, exciting moments that lift a person above the monotonous humdrum of daily existence are few. In the world they are often compensated for in drink, brawling, and loose living. Many, however, have found that Christianity offers them a similar release, and that worshiping God can even become ecstatic. The gift of tongues produces much spiritual satisfaction for many people, and non-Pentecostals should be cautious, as Paul himself recommends, about for-bidding others to speak in tongues (1 Co. 14:39).

How does speaking in tongues happen? Here is a firsthand testimony of a Latin American Pentecostal, which might well be considered typical of the tongues experience:

One time I was praying in a meeting. I believed very little in this matter of tongues, and had doubts. But on May 20, 1967, in a prayer meeting in church, as I was praying in a very concentrated way, all of a sudden I felt as if someone had turned a very strong searchlight on me and I was burning. I was going to speak in Spanish, but couldn't. I couldn't see anything but flames of fire all around me, and I felt as if I were burning. Then I began to speak in tongues—I was conscious, but I was in ecstasy.[6]

Some non-Pentecostals do forbid speaking in tongues on the grounds that they are not an appropriate gift for the church today. The Scofield Bible, which has been translated into Spanish, says in its note on 1 Corinthians 14:1 that "tongues and sign gifts are to cease," and many sincere Evangelicals believe it. It is not my purpose here to argue whether they are right or wrong. They are entitled to their opinion, although their attitude toward those who disagree with them should be one of love and tolerance.

But others say that while tongues might be appropriate today, Pentecostals in Latin America are abusing them like the Corinthians did, and to the degree that they need to be reprimanded and corrected. Whether they are or not is largely a matter of personal judgment. My own opinion is that for the most part this is not true. My understanding of the problem dealt with in 1 Corinthians 12-14 is that the Corinthians were dividing Christians into first-class and second-class categories on the basis of whether they had the gift of tongues or not.

The Corinthians' mistake was that they tended to make tongues the most important spiritual gift, a mistake which I personally have not observed in a general way among Latin American Pentecostals, although obviously the temptation to fall into that error is there, and cases might be cited to prove that some have gone off that deep end. Where this has happened, someone needs to exhort and reprimand these brethren, but in the Spirit.

Also, according to 1 Corinthians 14, tongues

must be accompanied by interpretation if they are used as a vehicle of communicating truths from God to the congregation as prophecy also does. This is true, but Paul goes on to say that if no interpreter is present, tongues should be used "to speak to himself and to God." (1 Co. 14:28) My understanding is that this is exactly what Pentecostals are doing when they pray in unison, some praying in tongues. They could do the same thing equally as effectively if they were at home in their private devotions, but the instructions in 1 Corinthians could hardly be limited to that.

So much for my brief apology for tongues in the Pentecostal liturgy. Let me simply repeat what I have said before: just because the Pentecostals do it, it doesn't mean that all Christians have to do it. Experience has shown that tongues are beyond doubt the most threatening aspect of Pentecostalism for non-Pentecostals. All right, even without tongues (one out of eight sub points in only one chapter of the book), Pentecostals have discovered many other secrets of church growth that can be applied by Christians who prefer not to speak in tongues. If only because of tongues someone says, "I want nothing to do with the Pentecostals," I'm afraid they have thrown out the baby with the bath water.

7. *The music.* One of the most unreal things I saw when I was first being introduced to Latin American Pentecostalism was an orchestra of about 500 members with the basic instruments being guitars, mandolins, and accordions. Not a pipe organ in the place! But a pipe organ never sounded like those 500 instruments.

Some will respond that they prefer a pipe organ in church any time. I would agree, as long as pipe organs are producing culturally-relevant liturgies that align people to the church and to Jesus Christ. To many Latin Americans, guitars and accordions are more attractive than pipe organs. It would be extremely difficult to classify one more "biblical" than the other. A more important question is: which sounds better to our people?

Clapping the hands in rhythm to the music is common in Pentecostal services in Latin America. This increases personal participation in the liturgy, raises the noise level several decibels, and heightens the tone of the drama. One of the severe structural problems that the Brazilian architects encountered while building the gigantic 25,000-seat auditorium for the Brazil for Christ Church in Sao Paulo related directly to this. The roof had to be designed with more than average care. If the huge span was to cover an airplane hangar or a warehouse it wouldn't have been that difficult. But the sound waves from 25,000 Brazilian Pentecostals clapping in unison could have produced the effect of troops marching over a bridge. The problems have been surmounted, however, and at this writing, the roof is nearing completion.

Indigenous Pentecostal hymnology is developing at different rates in different places. There is no such thing as a uniform Latin American musical style. Mexican, Bolivian, Brazilian, and Argentine music is all quite distinct. Some Pentecostal groups are working on this, but perhaps not as rapidly as one might expect. Even so, the translations of some of the Anglo-Saxon hymns are often sung to a Latin beat that might stun Charles Wesley if he were to hear what has happened to his music.

8. *The preaching.* Pentecostal preaching in Latin America is quite distinct from the monologues which characterize most of the traditional churches. The Pentecostal preacher enters into a kind of dialogue with his audience. The sermon is an experience for those who listen, as they respond with loud shouts of approval which surge up like waves breaking over the seashore. The preachers know just how much inflection to give to their voices, which phrases to repeat, which questions to ask, and when to pause so that the congregation can respond at the appropriate moment. Years of experience have made Pentecostal preachers some of the finest of all Latin American orators. They are superb communicators.

The preachers do all they can to identify with their people when they are on the platform. Their simple dress, their monosyllabic Spanish, and their style of delivery are all designed for this purpose. In the Brazil for Christ Church, Manoel de Melo has even done away with a pulpit so that nothing will stand between him and his congregation. He paces back and forth on the huge platform, microphone in hand, while he preaches.

Pentecostal preachers have little difficulty in communicating spiritual truth in meaningful terms, well-suited to the particular level of understanding of their people. Their sermons may seem to a casual observer to be rather thin, but if so the standard of judgment might not reflect the preacher's own purpose. Pentecostal preaching is not intellectual, but emotional; it is not rational, but experiential; it is not exegetical, but allegorical; it is not doctrinal, but practical; it is not directed as much to the head as to the heart. The result of hearing Pentecostal preaching is not that you learn more, but rather that you feel better.

Some non-Pentecostals have sincerely been worried about this. They have felt that the lack of theological depth will endanger the whole church. I confess that for some time I, too, was burdened that the Pentecostals did not have as much theological sophistication as others of us would have liked. But, as Nida points out, we should beware of hasty judgments. He says, "A more careful analysis will often reveal something far more relevant than may have been thought at first." [7]

The themes of Pentecostal preaching, while not drawing on much church history, philosophy, or systematic theology, do relate directly to where the people are living today. The pastor is not a bookish man who spends hours preparing well-structured sermons in his library-study. He is rather a man of the people who spends more time on the streets and in the homes than on sermonizing. Thus, when he preaches he might not go as deeply into the text as his counterpart in more traditional churches, but he rarely misses the mark as to relevance to where his listeners are living that very day. A homiletics professor might not grade him "A" on the sermon, but the people will leave feeling blessed, spiritually nourished, and motivated to serve God as well as possible for another week. In other words, his preaching has been successful.

These eight features of Pentecostal worship add up to a culturally-relevant liturgy. Pentecostals have very positive feelings about what goes on in their church services, and consequently they bring others in with them. The main reason they have such positive feelings, is, very simply, because it's fun to go to church.

9

Praying for the Sick

I cannot recall ever meeting an evangelical Christian who doubted God's ability to heal sickness without human medical aid. As a matter of fact, most of my friends have prayed for sick persons at one time or another, and they can testify to actual cases of healing. They are entirely familiar with Jesus' healing ministry, with Peter and John's experience with the lame man at the gate called Beautiful, and with Paul's extraordinary healing of the sick on the island of Malta.

It is all the more curious, therefore, when some of these same evangelical Christians so strongly oppose the element of divine healing in Pentecostal churches. Next to speaking in tongues, divine healing seems to be the most severe point of tension between Pentecostals and non-Pentecostals in Latin America.

I can say this with some authority, because only a decade ago I was one of the non-Pentecostals who militantly opposed divine healing campaigns. I clearly recall the visit of Puerto Rican faith healer Raimundo Jiménez to our city of Cochabamba, Bolivia. He came soon after a city-wide crusade held by an Argentine evangelist and sponsored by all the Protestant churches in the city, including the Pentecostals. With a great deal of effort and expense in publicity, visitation, and physical arrangements, the Argentine was able to draw record-breaking crowds of slightly over 1,000 to the local basketball stadium.

A couple of weeks later the Pentecostals sponsored the second crusade on their own because the other, more traditional, churches would not join them. Since they didn't have money for a basketball stadium, they found a large, vacant lot. Before the week was up they had crowds of 5,000 standing patiently throughout the entire service.

I must have suffered from a combination of incredulity, envy, and perhaps just plain frustration at seeing those throngs of people gathering as a result of seemingly so little effort on the part of those who organized the crusade. With all our expertise, our crowds were peanuts in comparison. We, of course, warned people in our churches not to attend the Pentecostal crusade. We accused our rivals of sheep-stealing and false teaching (although we were hard-pressed when asked to explain just what was their heresy). But in spite of our counsel, virtually every member of our church attended some of the meetings. As if that wasn't bad enough, some of them were healed!

I vented my frustrations in a nasty article, published in a nationally-circulated Christian magazine. This brought down the wrath of many of my Pentecostal friends, and I was labeled as their "public enemy number one" for some time. Happily, I learned much from the Lord over the next few years, and the black mark beside my name has been largely erased. But having gone through these experiences, I can well understand the attitude of my non-Pentecostal brethren who are still where I was ten years ago.

At least I came out of the experience better than another non-Pentecostal scoffer in Mexico. One of the early leaders of the Apostolic Church of the Faith was Miguel García, a tall, thin barber who had proved to be an effective evanglist and who founded the church in Torreón, among others.

When he first arrived in Torreón in 1918, García was frequently invited to preach in the Methodist, Baptist, and Presbyterian churches there. Soon afterwards, however, the invitations abruptly ceased. He learned that the pastors were opposed to his teaching on two points: speaking in tongues and divine healing. So García started his own meetings.

One wealthy and prominent Evangelical decided to challenge García publicly. Every day at about the same time a paralyzed man would drag himself past the rich man's home. The rich man stopped him and asked him where he was going. "To García's meetings," he answered, "I want to be healed."

The rich man poked fun at him, and told him he was wasting his time. "I'll lose my neck before I ever see you healed," he said with a sneer. Just a few days later, however, the paralyzed man was walking normally. And the rich man? He died suddenly with an infection in his neck! Understandably, the outward opposition to García came to an abrupt halt.[1]

The moment of truth is almost unavoidable for non-Pentecostals in Latin America. With two-thirds of Evangelicals calling themselves Pentecostals, and with the percentage rising every year, what Pentecostals do there can't be ignored. It will not help to pretend the problem doesn't exist, like United States auto manufacturers did when competing dealers began to import German and Japanese cars. When needy men and women can find something in other churches that yours does not offer, when this is something good, and when it has biblical support, a great deal of honesty and open-mindedness is called for. Non-Pentecostals in Latin America would be well-advised to anticipate the coming moment of truth rather than let it take them by surprise.

In Guayaquíl, Ecuador, the reality of divine healing took many Christians by surprise. The story of the highly successful Foursquare crusade in Guayaquíl has been told in detail in chapters three and four. But one factor that contributed heavily to its success has not yet been mentioned: divine healing was one of the keys to baptizing 1,500 new Christians and planting seven new churches in six weeks.

The Foursquare missionary, Roberto Aguirre, had been led to believe by the other pastors in the city that they would cooperate in his crusade just as Aguirre had cooperated with theirs a few months previously. Then as the date approached the other pastors quietly began to back off. They had heard that the evangelist, who was coming from California was Roberto Espinoza, a faith healer. A meeting was called after Espinoza arrived, and not a single one of the other pastors showed up. The Foursquare leaders were sad, and rather nervous. They had already invested $1,000 for the stadium and $1,000 for the expenses of Espinoza and his wife. Since they could not depend on their skeptical brethren, they were forced to cast themselves entirely upon God.

God did not let them down. The very day before the meetings were to begin, the owner of a local radio station came to see Aguirre. Aguirre had never met the man and assumed he was coming for business reasons—to sell radio time. But the budget had already been overspent, and barely any advertising at all had been done for the crusade. Aguirre wondered how the radio man even knew there were going to be meetings in Guayaquíl.

The man was remarkably cordial, however, and said that he would like to offer his radio station to broadcast the services. "I'm sorry," Aguirre said, "but we have no money."

"Money is no problem," the radio man answered. "I have come to offer my radio time free. If you pay the expenses of the technician, you can have it."

It goes without saying that Aguirre could hardly believe his ears. Then he probed to find out what God had done to motivate the radio station owner.

Lo and behold, Aguirre discovered that the man had recently been healed through the prayers of a member of Aguirre's congregation! He was so grateful for renewed health that he wanted as many others as possible in Guayaquíl to have it as well.

The first night the crowd was disappointing. Fewer than 1,000 persons showed up. Roberto Espinoza prayed for the sick that night and four deaf people and twelve with hernias were healed. The whole thing was broadcast to Guayaquíl over the radio, and the news spread fast. Attendance the second night rose to 10,000; it was up to 20,000 by the end of the first week; and before the crusade ended, the number of people standing in the vast open field was estimated at between 35,000 and 40,000. Many dramatic healings took place, but more important "the Lord added to the church daily such as should be saved," in this case 1,500 in six weeks.[2]

Studies have shown that faith healing is a more universal characteristic of Latin American Pentecostals than other charismatic gifts, for example, speaking in tongues. In a survey of Pentecostal pastors in Chile, Lalive found that whereas only fifty-seven percent of them had spoken in tongues, a full ninety-eight percent had been instruments of divine healing.[3] It is necessary, therefore, to understand the role of praying for the sick if one is to uncover the dynamics of Pentecostalism in Latin America.

As we have pointed out many times, the Pentecostal message seems particularly relevant to the proletariat, the working lower classes of Latin America. These same lower classes have a saying that goes, *"enfermarse es un lujo"*—getting sick is a luxury. In many of the rural villages of Latin America medical aid is nonexistent, and in the cities few can squeeze the costs of medical and hospital bills into their skimpy budgets. The use of folk medicine is very common, and while it is at times remarkably helpful this is not always the case. Many go beyond folk medicine to witchcraft, and it is painful to admit that some Christians, perhaps more than we would want to think, turn to witch doctors because they do not know where else to go in their desperation.

When common people like this hear that faith in God alone can produce healing without electrocardiograms, prescriptions, injections, or even fetishes, it is no wonder they are attracted. The physical suffering that is so much a part of today's Latin America becomes a strong motivating force to bring men and women under the hearing of the message the Pentecostals preach.

No one should assume that, because of this, physical healing has become more important in Pentecostal preaching than spiritual salvation. This brings us to the matter of priorities, a point which non-Pentecostals often raise. They tend to say, "They may preach some spectacular kind of bodily healing, but we preach Christ and Him crucified as salvation from sin." This creates a dichotomy which may be helpful for polemical purposes, but which Pentecostals do not feel. There is no question in the minds of any Pentecostals I know that the eternal dimension of the salvation of the soul is a higher priority than the temporal dimension of the healing of the body. But to them it is not an either/or, but a both/and situation.

When Read, Monterroso, and Johnson wrote *Latin American Church Growth* they were concerned with this problem. During their field research they often probed deeply to discover what were true Pentecostal priorities. They found that a rather consistent thread of faith healing ran through the most successful of the evangelistic crusades, such as those held by Tommy Hicks in Argentina, A. A. Allen in Venezuela, and Morris Cerullo in Uruguay. But they make a point of adding that "In all these campaigns, the principal element is the preaching of the gospel. Healing is presented as just one of the blessings that God provided in Christ and His saving work." [4]

To move to a specific case, a Chilean pastor tells of a family that brought their mother to him with a paralyzed leg. They sought him out because he had a small truck, and they asked him to take her to the hospital. The truck was broken and would require several hours to fix. So the pastor said, "Listen, I will gladly take you to the hospital, but it will take time to fix the truck. But I also know that we, the Pentecostals, can cure your mother."

They wanted nothing to do with Pentecostals; they simply wanted transportation so they could get competent medical help. The pastor then made the following proposition: "We will fix the truck, but while we are doing it, the brothers will come to pray. If by the time we are ready to go your mother is cured, will you agree to be converted to the Lord?"

They reluctantly agreed. When the truck was fixed and ready to go, the Christians picked up the mother they had been praying for, and she moved her leg. The paralysis was gone. She had been cured! From that time on the whole family began coming to the Pentecostal services.[5]

This typical story shows that Pentecostals are interested in the ultimate effect that divine healing will have on eternal salvation. Among Pentecostals in Colombia, Palmer found that the consistent attitude toward faith healing is something like this Pentecostal pastor put it: "The object of healing for the unsaved is as bait. It attracts their attention to the power of Christ, Who can also save."[6] Healing, although a good thing, is not considered an end in itself by most Latin American Pentecostals. It is for the most part a manifestation of the power of God that will ultimately attract unbelievers to Jesus Christ as Savior and Lord. Healing is, thus, an effective evangelistic tool which only incidentally brings temporal blessings.

Some Pentecostals go to unfortunate extremes. Gaxiola tells of some early trends in Mexico that declared the use of any kind of medicine, including aspirin and Mentholatum, to be conclusive evidence of lack of faith, and consequently grounds for excommunication.[7] Palmer found that in Colombia, while the United Pentecostals would permit Alka-Seltzer and vitamins, they strictly prohibited the use of doctors or strong medicines in the past.

This attitude is changing in Colombia, however.[8] It is not typical of Latin American Pentecostals in general. Most Pentecostals do not prohibit the use of modern medicine. If doctors are available and money is on hand to pay the bills, ordinary healing processes are encouraged, although always accompanied by prayer. But when medical help is not available for one reason or another, the gift of healing is brought into play.

A fine distinction is made by some Pentecostals between the gift of healing and the gift of miracles. Healing is the supernatural intervention of the power of God in cases that apparently could also be cured by doctors in hospitals, if the patients could afford them. Miracles, on the other hand, involve cases that have deteriorated beyond the possibilities of medical science. A virus infection or an abscess or dysentery are cared for by the gift of healing. Cancer or congenital mental retardation need the gift of miracles. Both are present among Latin American Pentecostals, but healing is much more common than miracles.

The most publicized cases of divine healing are usually those that fall into the category of miracles. A little boy who was healed in the great Tommy Hicks crusade in Buenos Aires in 1954 received city-wide press coverage, and this in turn drew multitudes to the meetings. Some considered it the turning point of the crusade. It just so happened that when the mother brought this three-year-old boy with a brace on his deformed leg, four physicians were on the platform. After prayer, the brace was removed and in plain sight of thousands of people the boy walked, then ran, then jumped. The people began to cheer. Then one of the physicians moved over to the boy. The mother looked up at him. Incredibly, he was the very same doctor who had fitted the brace and told her that the boy would need it for the rest of his life.

The emotion of the moment was so high that both the mother and the doctor began to weep profusely. When he had examined the leg, he dropped to his knees and said, "I want this Christ. I want to be saved." According to Hicks, this doctor and also one of his colleagues accepted Christ that night.[9] Hicks was thankful for the healing, but typically, even more so that the healing had brought these two men into eternal salvation.

Divine healing in crusades such as Hicks, Espinoza, and Jiménez conducted is sporadic. The crusades come and go, but the churches stay on. How, then, do the churches handle praying for the sick on a more regular basis?

A good bit of the day-by-day healing happens in the sick rooms. Pentecostals in Latin America take quite literally the verse in James that says, "Is anyone among you sick? Let him call for the elders of the church, and let them pray over him, anointing him with oil in the name of the Lord; and the prayer offered in faith will restore the one who is sick." (James 5:14-15) I wouldn't be surprised if some Pentecostals pray for the sick as often as Presbyterians repeat the Lord's Prayer. And they continue to believe in it because they all have seen it work so frequently.

The liturgy in many Pentecostal churches includes faith healing as a matter of routine. In the Jotabeche Church in Chile healing occurs after the main service. The pastor remains in the front of the sanctuary, and a line forms by the platform. Some persons simply want to greet the pastor, some have brought him a gift, and others ask him to pray for a personal problem or for healing. When the prayer involves healing, the believer will kneel, and the pastor will place his hand upon the head.

Much more prominent as a part of the liturgy

is the healing service in the Brazil for Christ Church in Sao Paulo. There, when the proper point in the liturgy arrives, Pastor Manoel de Melo ceremoniously removes his suit jacket and puts on a double-breasted white coat. He then announces what particular sickness he will deal with. He might be treating head problems that night, for example. If so, he will go into a lengthy description of every conceivable physical malady that can occur from the neck up, and invite anyone suffering from one of these problems to come forward. Out of the congregation of up to 8,000, hundreds will respond until the space in front of the platform is filled.

The treatment begins with an explanation of the medical importance of the head, followed by a brief sermon on divine healing. This is designed to build up weak faith to the point where it may be exercised effectively. When this is over, de Melo has the entire congregation stand.

"Does the church believe that Jesus can heal?" he asks.

"Yes, the church believes that Jesus can heal!" comes back the response from thousands of people.

He repeats it several times, until it sounds like the waves of the ocean breaking over rocks. Then he leads in the prayer of faith for the sick, and moves out among the sick people, touching their heads and praying for them one by one. He concludes by having the congregation repeat after him the final prayer, with hands uplifted.

Edward Murphy, who has done special research on the Brazil for Christ Church, was present at one service where de Melo dismissed all the sick people but one. He took one elderly man up on the platform with him, and said, "I kept this man here on purpose. He has a serious problem. He is blind. This sickness is of the devil. When I put my hand on him, I felt heat in my hand. I know the Lord Jesus is curing him right this instant. He is now being healed."

The congregation broke out into applause, and the man sat down. Then, to heighten the drama, de Melo called the man back, and said, "He was healed. Now he can see," and he had the man follow him back and forth across the platform.

By that time, Murphy says, "The people went almost hysterical with joy, clapping, raising their hands to Jesus, and praising Him for His healing power." [10]

Notice that de Melo said, "This is of the devil." That brings up one more point that needs to be mentioned in a chapter on faith healing, namely exorcism. Demonic power is not recognized and dealt with in many of the slower-growing non-Pentecostal churches in Latin America, but it is a frequent subject of sermon, discussion, and action in the Pentecostal churches.

As far as I have been able to determine, the only detailed analysis of this aspect of Latin American Pentecostalism was done by missionary Harmon Johnson in a work entitled *Authority Over the Spirits: Brazilian Spiritism and Evangelical Church Growth.* [11] Johnson enviably combines the objectivity of a scholar, the personal involvement of a Pentecostal (Assemblies of God), and many years of first-hand experience in Brazil in this definitive study.

By choosing Brazil, Johnson has moved into the territory where the power of the devil may be more directly and universally felt than in any other Latin American country with the exception of Haiti. While all Brazilians are not spiritists, virtually all of their lives have been touched at one point or another by this religion of the devil. Johnson's conclusions, therefore, can be applied much further afield than just Brazil.

Although written with great sensitivity, one of Johnson's findings amounts to a severe rebuke for non-Pentecostals. The most typical reaction of non-Pentecostals to spiritism has been one of polemics, and the kind of polemics which indicates that they do not take the validity of spiritism very seriously. "It is difficult to see," Johnson says, "how any spiritist would be interested in reading through any book which concentrates on the negative aspects of spiritism, and which talks mostly about fraud, superstition, credulity, and the triviality of a religion to which he has committed his whole life." [12]

It is no wonder that non-Pentecostal churches are winning so few people from spiritism in Brazil, relatively speaking. Spiritism is not simply ignorance, superstition, and chicanery. A Christianity which does not recognize it as a manifestation of the powers of darkness will continue to be impotent in this particular field of evangelism.

The Pentecostal churches in Brazil go to the heart of the matter and recognize spiritism for what it is—supernatural, demonic activity. They believe that the miracles worked by spirits are real, but that they can be traced to Satan. Consequently, their evangelistic approach to spiritists stresses the power encounter, and they are not afraid to pit the power of God against the power of Satan any more than Elijah was when he faced the priests of Baal on Mt. Carmel. Their message is that of "Christ the Victor," and a common theme in preaching is deliverance from the powers of Satan. This is the kind of message that spiritists understand and respond to.

The experience of Giberto Stevao, a leader of Umbanda spiritism before his conversion, is considered by Johnson to be typical. Stevao was converted; he had received the Pentecostal experience; but it took twelve days for him to face his power encounter. He had gone to bed, read his New Testament, and turned out the light. But he could not sleep. The wind whistling through the bushes outside produced a great fear in him until he was seized with chills. He tried to scream for help, but could not speak. He was paralyzed with fear. He knew that a demon, a "spirit of rebellion," had entered his room. Then he heard a nearby voice saying "chi-chi-chi."

Stevao says, "I cried in my heart, 'What shall I do, Jesus?' But it appeared to me that He was far away... I began to cry, 'The blood of Jesus has power. I rebuke you, Satan, I cast you out by the blood of Jesus.' But it seemed like I was saying vain words. No result."

The encounter continued, unabated, throughout the night. Stevao's soul had become the battleground for a ferocious spiritual struggle. But as time went by, courage and faith began to build up. Finally Stevao dared to cry out, "Satan, you lying enemy! I am and always will be a friend and companion of the Lord Jesus Christ! Go, and the blood of Jesus Christ crush your head!" With that, the demon left, and Stevao had been liberated.[13]

Without building the power encounter into your

doctrine and practice, you cannot be effective in reaching the millions of Latin Americans who are subject to demonic activity of one kind or another. Exorcism of demons is a part of the ministry of almost all Latin American Pentecostal churches, and Johnson feels that, at least in Brazil, it is the most important key to Pentecostal church growth.[14]

Some non-Pentecostal churches, happily, are listening. Many more need to if they are to increase their effectiveness. Praying for the sick and casting out demons are New Testament practices which should not hastily be pushed outside of the sphere of Christian experience. The influence of secularism and scientism has dulled the edge of Christian sensitivity to these matters, undoubtedly to Satan's advantage. We can be thankful that Pentecostals in Latin America, among others, are reminding us that, in the twentieth century as well as in the first, we can preach a gospel of power, and that Christ is Liberator.

10

Are Pentecostals on a "Social Strike"?

Because of their phenomenal numerical growth, Pentecostals in Latin America have become the object of several sociological studies of one kind or another. One of the best of these was commissioned by the World Council of Churches and carried out in Chile by Swiss sociologist Christian Lalive. His findings are reported in the book, *Haven of the Masses*, which has been quoted several times already.

Lalive is a friend of the Pentecostals and has many good things to say about them. But at one point he consistently lets considerable irritation show through. He is concerned that Pentecostals are not actively involved in promoting social (as contrasted to personal) reform in Latin America. Lalive's study convinced him that:

> Pentecostalism teaches its initiates withdrawal and passivity in socio-political matters, limited only by the commandment to be submissive to authority. . . . These components make it in the last analysis a force for order rather than an element of progress, a defender of the status quo and not a promoter of change.[1]

Lalive is very outspoken when he states that in his judgment, this aspect of the Pentecostal movement is "most regrettable." He sees Chilean Pentecostals aligned politically nearer the conservatives than to any other political grouping, and considers this "its point of weakness." In another place he accuses Pentecostals of going on a "sociopolitical strike." [2] All this, of course, reveals Lalive's own political bias, obviously somewhat further to the left than he found Chilean Pentecostals to be.

To balance the picture, an equally competent sociologist, Emilio Willems of Vanderbilt University, takes a much more positive view of the way that the Pentecostal Church has affected social change in Brazil and Chile. He contends that the Pentecostals have in effect challenged the status quo, and cites examples of social change that can be traced to their influence in one way or another.[3] Winston Elliot, in a sociocultural study of Pentecostals in Sonora, Mexico, found that by functioning as a protest group, the Pentecostal church was making a substantial contribution to social change.[4] Most of this, however, is indirect. No one would classify Latin American Pentecostals as social activists.

Now, at this point I could go on for several pages describing sociological trends and ideological biases. But this is not the purpose of raising the question. This is a book on the growth of the Pentecostal churches in Latin America. What the social stance of these churches should or should not be is a fascinating subject, but it must be debated elsewhere. We here are basically interested in whether the socio-political position of Latin American Pentecostals in general helps or hinders the growth of their churches.

In other words, are Pentecostal churches in Latin America growing so phenomenally *because* of or *in spite of* their social position?

I am steadily becoming more and more convinced that the social stance of Pentecostals is a positive factor in church growth. It is not the only positive factor, of course, as the rest of this book hopefully proves. Furthermore, whether it is beneficial to the socio-economic development of Latin America across the board is another matter that I am prepared to debate, but not in this book. I am reasonably sure, however, that it helps, not hinders, numerical church growth.

Perhaps I would not have dared state this so categorically if it had not been for the recent publication of Dean Kelley's remarkable book, *Why Conservative Churches are Growing*. His book is written about North American churches, but his findings may turn out to apply equally well to Latin American churches—or churches almost anywhere for that matter.

Pentecostals, as we have mentioned, are not known in Latin America for their involvement in the battle for justice and brotherhood. Whereas they put great emphasis on cleaning up one's personal life, they do not seem equally concerned about cleaning up the world around them. Lalive suggests they should. He wants them to alter their political ethic. He wants Pentecostals to develop a new ethic of involvement and activism. "The believer would join the political parties and the trade unions ... " if Lalive had his way. He desires that they participate directly in the transformation of their country.[5]

There is no question that if the millions of Pentecostals in such countries as Brazil and Chile were to follow Lalive's advice, they could garner sufficient power to bring about vast social change. But what Lalive does not seem to be concerned about, and here is where Dean Kelley comes in, is that by doing so, they might actually *lose social strength*. To use a biblical analogy, they might end up selling their birthright for a mess of pottage like Esau did.

The key phrase in Kelley's book is "social strength." He found that churches in the United States which have the greatest social strength are the ones increasing in membership. Conversely the socially weak ones tend to diminish.[6] On a continuum of twenty-seven religious groups in the United States, ranging from the strongest to the weakest, Evangelicals and Pentecostals together rank third behind Black Muslims and Jehovah's Witnesses.[7]

How do religious groups accumulate social strength?

Kelley answers this question with an elaborate chart which we will not try to reproduce here.[8] Very simply, he found that the stricter a religious group is, the more social strength it gains. The

— 140 —

strongest groups, for example, are the ones which believe that they have the truth, that others are in error, and that dialogue is a waste of time. They believe in heresy and excommunication. They do not hesitate to persuade others of their faith with a missionary zeal.

When it comes to social involvement and participation in the great political forces of the day, Kelley confirms what Lalive found in Chile: "There is something intrinsically conservative about the religious enterprise." [9] But their disagreement arises in the interpretation of this fact. Kelley says what Lalive probably would not: "This is not necessarily bad." Kelley even calls the conserving tendency of religious organizations "basically a healthy and valuable trait, which gives coherence and continuity to human society." [10]

All of this drives us to a deeper sociological question: What are churches for, anyway?

Before answering this question, let us pause to remind ourselves that we are not here discussing the biblical basis of evangelism and church planting. We are asking sociological questions, and therefore we must answer them in sociological terms. Committed Christians know that the Bible has other, more essential, answers that we have discussed in other chapters.

Men and women in society look to churches for one supreme function: to provide them with a satisfying explanation of *the meaning of life in ultimate terms.* [11] Meaning is altogether as deep a human need as shelter or sex or food. Christian churches can meet this need, and meet it well. Part of the meaning preached by Christians involves nothing less than eternal salvation.

Some think that social activism should also

be a function of the church. But perhaps the time has come to ask whether social involvement is really within the competence of Christian churches after all. As one leafs back through the pages of history, he finds that Christianity has not made a particularly sensational score in producing social change. One can find exceptions here and there, and Christian individuals who have been leaders of reform movements abound. But churches, as social institutions, have done a much better job at providing ultimate meaning than they have in tearing down and building up social structures.

This has been a source of considerable consternation to many sincere Christians, and also a source of some ridicule and criticism from the enemies of Christianity. Now, however, Dean Kelley tells us we might have worried too much. He says that churches which set out to benefit society more by patriotic preaching, welfare services, or social action may be in for a surprise. If by doing this they do not perform as well in making life meaningful for their members, they ironically end up benefiting society *less*.[12] They have sold their birthright for a mess of pottage.

Now, let's apply Kelley's findings to Latin America. Across the board, studies have found that of all Latin American Protestants, Pentecostals seem the least interested in becoming involved in the great social issues of the day. Methodists, Presbyterians, Anglicans, Lutherans, Baptists, and others rate much higher in social concern. But, as we have seen, they also rate much lower in church growth, and by inference they rate lower in social strength.

One of the most extreme cases I have come

across is Donald Palmer's report of the Jesus Only Pentecostal groups in Colombia. He made a special point to find out what their attitude toward social issues was. He asked a cross section of pastors the following question: "Do you believe that the Evangelical church ought to concern itself more with the social problems of the country, and declare itself with respect to these problems?"

Non-Pentecostal pastors immediately responded yes. But United Pentecostal pastors were unanimous in their opinion that Christians should not be involved in social issues.[13] More specifically, they opposed any Christian involvement with organized athletics, politics or labor unions.[14] Most, but not all of them, even refuse to cast their ballot in national elections.

If anyone is on a social strike, it would be the United Pentecostals in Colombia. That is not their only mark of seemingly excessive strictness, however. Women may not cut their hair, and their apparel must be up to the most rigid standards of modesty. Members may not attend dances, theaters of any kind, or soccer matches. Not only television, but even radio and secular music are also considered worldly. The United Pentecostal Church Manual says, "We warn all of our believers to abstain from any of these practices in the interest of spiritual growth and the soon coming of the Lord for His church."[15]

It would be easy to draw the conclusion that such standards would quickly render the United Pentecostal Church irrelevant to contemporary Colombian society. Many observers, as a matter of fact, do. But wiser considerations will avoid hasty judgments. One of these wiser men is Justo González, Jr., who discusses the Pentecostals' separation from the world and their non-participation in politics, but then says, "On the other hand, it is difficult to see how a movement that is totally irrelevant to the human situation can have the surprising growth that is characteristic of Pentecostalism.[16] Such behavior also fits Dean Kelley's criteria of social strength.

It might well be, therefore, that the strictness of the United Pentecostals in Colombia is actually one of the *causes* of the fact that they are the largest and fastest growing church in the nation.

Intuitively Pentecostals understand that their resources are limited, and that decisions as to the degree of social involvement boil down ultimately to a matter of priorities.

No one has expressed this sensitivity to priorities more thoughtfully than Melvin Hodges, the Latin American Secretary for the Assemblies of God. Hodges says, "Let us put first things first." He goes on:

> There is nothing as important as getting men's hearts right with God. The center must be put right before the periphery can be corrected. To try to remedy peripheral conditions leaving the heart unchanged is useless and deceiving. When a man is truly converted, he seeks a better life for himself and his family. One has only to observe the families of Evangelical Christians over a period of a few years to note that spiritual conversion leads to improvement in every aspect of a convert's life.[17]

If spiritual conversion is not continually articulated and practiced as the first priority, a church is in danger of becoming nominal. Social strength can diminish almost imperceptibly at first, until it is too late. One of the large Latin American Pentecostal churches, for example, has recently joined the World Council of Churches, expressing the hope that they can teach the W.C.C. something about evangelism, while learning from the W.C.C. something about social action. This move will bear close watching. It is not difficult to predict that the relationship may ultimately lead to a loss of social strength and a leveling off of the rate of church growth. One can only hope that this church has not joined others in selling its birthright.

When Pentecostal churches blur the clear line of priorities that Hodges has drawn, when they become ashamed of their lower-class members and seek more "respectability," when they introduce more "dignity" into their liturgy, and when they decide to "upgrade" the educational standards of the ministry, trouble may be just down the road. Building more and more social activism into their church programs becomes another step toward an almost certain sapping of social strength.

Now all this should not be interpreted to mean that Pentecostalism has no social influence at all in Latin America. Their very strictness, according to Kelley's thesis, should build social strength. All Pentecostal watchers admit that it does, although it often is not the kind of social strength that some of the observers would like if they had their own way.

Pentecostals have at times been accused of holding doctrines of dualism or docetism. Dualism means that you make an absolute distinction between body and soul. Docetism means that you even go so far as to negate the reality of the body. To dualists the soul, or the spiritual side of man, is of supreme importance, and what happens to the body is of no concern at all.

Anyone who has read the chapter "Praying for the Sick" knows that Latin American Pentecostals hardly merit the accusations of dualism or docetism. *Bodily* healing is very important for them. Some of them, I understand, even go so far as to claim that the healing of the body was included in the atonement of Christ on the cross, a doctrine that leaves much to be desired, but one that at least does not indicate a neglect of the body. Pentecostals believe in the whole man, and are vitally interested in him, body and soul. Here is how one Pentecostal preacher expressed it in a sermon:

> Sin has two aspects—spiritual and physical. Christ healed spiritually and physically; I repeat: spiritually *and* physically. We have come here not just with a gospel of words, but also of demonstrations ... Christ saves and heals today just as He did then. He died to save; He lives to heal ...[18]

A fascinating anecdote about the social impact of the gospel is told of Willis Hoover, the founder of the Chilean Methodist Pentecostal Church. Apparently, his ministry in Valparaíso had some special attraction for thieves. As some of the thieves would sneak out for their nightly rounds, they would hear the joyful sound of the Methodist Pentecostals, listen for a while, and become convicted of sin. The local police department, concerned that they could not seem to keep track of many of their suspects, eventually traced them to Hoover's meetings.

Then they did something that as far as I know is unprecedented in evangelistic annals. They sent Hoover a New Year's card containing the photographs of twenty-four criminals. The genial message suggested that these photographs appropriately should be filed in the church. They no longer belonged in the police station![19] The Valparaíso police force, for one, did not consider the social impact of the Pentecostal message a matter for debate at that point.

The *Congregacao Crista* in Sao Paulo have their own social program well organized. About 100 of their women have joined forces in a group called "ministry of piety," and they function like a team of social workers. They have set up an office in the main church building, and they consider applications from members of their church who need help of some kind or another. If circumstances warrant, they will provide funds for food, fuel, clothing, or household items. They will care for some medical bills. They will even make capital loans for small businesses. This is all done as to the Lord, and donors remain strictly anonymous.[20]

These Brazilian Pentecostals take seriously Paul's admonition to the Galatian Christians, "So then, while we have opportunity, let us do good to all men, and especially to those who are of the household of the faith." (Gal. 6:10) One of the very things that makes the Pentecostal faith so attractive to the Brazilian masses is knowing that other members of God's family are concerned for a person's social as well as his spiritual needs.

These needs are cared for even more remarkably in the Assemblies of God churches in Brazil. The church complex (mother and daughters) in

Sao Paulo, for example, runs a tile factory, provides medical and dental services, runs a primary and secondary school, teaches Portuguese, typing, music, and sewing, and operates a hospital, an old people's home, and a Bible school. "God cares for our souls;" they say, "we have to care for bodies." [21]

Evidence shows that Pentecostals in Latin America are not on a "social strike," as some might think. They know that the gospel is relevant to the whole man, and to man in society. Their approach to solving social problems might differ considerably from that of some Christians in the more traditional denominations, but it is no less a concern for humanity. Since they have not allowed their concern for humanity to degenerate into humanism, however, they have conserved social strength. Therein, they have become an instrument in the hands of the Holy Spirit to bring the message of liberation to Latin American people in a highly relevant and effective way.

11

Pentecostals
in Non-Pentecostal Churches

The Latin American Congress on Evangelization, held in Bogotá in 1969, was the largest and most spectacular gathering of Latin American evangelical leaders to date. Over 900 delegates from every Latin American republic except Cuba met to develop strategies to increase evangelistic fervor and effectiveness over the whole continent.

At the Bogotá Congress, Latin American Evangelicals for the first time became aware of a new and highly significant development within Protestant churches, Rubén Lores, President of the prestigious Latin American Biblical Seminary of San José, Costa Rica, stirred the delegates with an epoch-making address in which he described the entrance of Pentecostal practices into some non-

Pentecostal churches. Many delegates congratulated Lores for his courage in dealing on such a high level with an obviously controversial topic. Others, predictably, expressed strong displeasure at the message. Events since 1969, however, have shown how prophetic Lores' address really was.

Lores called the charismatic movement in Latin America a fulfillment of Joel's prophecy as quoted by Peter on Pentecost:

And it shall be in the last days, God says,
That I will pour forth of My Spirit upon all mankind;
And your sons and your daughters shall prophesy,
And your young men shall see visions,
And your old men shall dream dreams . . .

Lores traced the history of the charismatic movement in the United States over recent decades through three streams: classical Pentecostals, "Penteprotestants," and "Pentecatholics." He described the renewing power of these charismatic manifestations in the churches in dramatically optimistic terms. Then he said that churches in Puerto Rico, Guatemala, Costa Rica, Colombia, Chile, Argentina, and Brazil had also been renewed through the charismatic movement.[1]

This brought it close to home for the delegates. Too close for some. Since then, one of the questions foremost in the minds of Latin American Evangelicals has been: To what extent has the Pentecostal movement spilled over the boundaries of the Pentecostal denominations and entered the more traditional churches? We will attempt to answer that with the data we have. We will also zero in on the questions more directly related to this book. What *effect* has this had on the non-

Pentecostal churches where Pentecostal practices have entered? Has this, in fact, helped churches to grow?

During the 1950's the Roman Catholic persecution of the Protestants in Colombia was so fierce that it became one of the notorious examples of violation of human rights in our day. Hundreds of Protestants were brutally murdered for their faith. Many others of them fled into the uninhabited parts of Colombia in order to conserve both their faith and their lives. One of these, deep in the forest region of northern Colombia, would ride out on horseback to preach and sell Bibles in the small, backwoods towns.

He couldn't have suspected it at the time, but one of the Bibles he sold eventually sparked what has been called a "spontaneous combustion" movement to Christ. A local bartender, named Victor Landero,[2] who also managed a stable of prostitutes, bought the Bible, read it, and was converted in 1957. He dismissed his prostitutes, sold his bar, and worked on his small farm for a while. Then he bought a new farm upriver in order to enter an unevangelized area. Many of his new neighbors were converted. He was so excited that he asked God to help him feed his family so he could give more time to Christian work. Eventually only two days a week were required to keep the farm producing. The other five were God's, and they were used in effective evangelism.

There were no missionaries or other Colombian Christians directing this movement. God here had the opportunity to instruct these new believers with only the Bible and the Holy Spirit. He did it in ways more reminiscent of the book of Acts than perhaps of the typical contemporary missionary handbook.

One night Victor Landero had a vivid dream of a certain hut in the woods, which he had never seen before.[3] A clear voice said to him, "The people in that hut are dying without Christ because no one ever told them of Him." It took some time to do it, but months later Victor started out through the woods with no idea where he was going. After only two days, he came into a clearing and saw the hut of which he had dreamed. He knocked on the door, met the family, and told them why he had come.

The woman of the house was speechless. Only three nights previously, she had dreamed a strange dream. She saw her house full of people with a stranger talking to them out of a book. The word "gospel" came to her in her dream, although she had never heard the word before.

News spread, and that evening twenty-four neighbors came to hear the stranger talk out of the book. Every one of them received Christ. The next night ten more came, and they, too, were converted. All of them later continued in the apostles' doctrine, fellowship, breaking of bread and prayers, just as they did in the book of Acts. Landero went home rejoicing.

Soon a seeming obstacle appeared on the horizon. A false cult had begun moving through the area in 1961, preaching heretical doctrine. Victor Landero became so disturbed at his inability to refute these errors intellectually that he began to take frequent trips to a secluded place in the forest to fast and pray. He spent many hours there crying bitterly before God. Some other believers joined him. One day something unusual happened. They were overcome with a sense of joy that they could not explain. They prayed through the night, and read the book of Acts to each other. After they had done this several times, spontaneously one of them spoke in tongues! Others soon began to do the same.

A type of charismatic movement had started in the Colombian forest, but it was a "spontaneous combustion" process. Obviously, this particular manifestation of the Spirit had come down from heaven. It was not something that had been taught to them by other Christians.

This happened here not *because of*, but *in spite of*, the missionaries. By this time, American missionaries from a non-Pentecostal mission had discovered the group and were encouraging it from time to time. But their first reaction to the outbreak of this charismatic movement was not favorable. They found themselves in a dilemma. The mission had a policy of allowing the local leadership to direct the work, and in this case the local leadership was leading the charismatic movement. They decided that the best approach would be to have a series of Bible studies on the Holy Spirit with the believers.

The Bible studies were designed to point out Pentecostal errors indirectly, without mentioning Pentecostalism at all. The effect was just the opposite, however. As one of the Colombian leaders expresses it, the Bible studies were just like throwing gasoline on the fire. Not only did the local believers gain more confidence in using the gifts they had been given, but the news of these gifts began to spread to other churches in the area.

Soon after the gift of tongues came the gift of interpretation. One of the first messages received through tongues and interpretation was a clear command to persevere in what they were doing. They received it as the voice of God. Then they started praying for the sick, and many were healed. A blind man received his sight. A paralytic began to walk for the first time. Young men saw visions, and old men dreamed dreams. Everyone was praising the Lord. Worries about the false cult evaporated when the Spirit began to show His power.

God gave some the gift of prophecy. A girl was having serious personal problems, but none of her friends were able to get her to admit them and confess her sin. At a regional Bible conference, however, a young fellow who did not know the girl received a prophecy from God. He stood up in a public meeting, and said, "Is Señorita so-and-so here?" Her heart came up in her throat! He named her problems specifically, and then gave her instructions from God as to how to deal with them. She fell to her knees in repentance, and the matter was cared for instantly. All were blessed, and the gift of prophecy had edified the body.

Witchcraft is common back in the Colombian forests, and the power of God is needed to deal with it. As in the case of Brazil, the power encounter between Jesus and the devil is taken very seriously. Manuel Sena, for example, had been a sorcerer before his conversion. Secretly he hid one of his metal fetishes, wrapped in a cloth, inside a jar, and put the jar in a storage box.

Although a Christian, the demons would not let him alone after that. In desperation he finally asked his brothers to help him, and they prayed for him one night. He was thrown to the ground by some demonic power, and while in a coma a strange voice came out of his mouth telling the others about the fetish. Sena later confessed that it was true.

The next day Victor Landero went home with him. His wife had also gone through a terrifying demonic experience the night before. She had felt a horrible fear of the box where the fetish was hidden. She had prayed, and as she did, their dog had started barking and rushing around the room as if someone were chasing him. Finally things calmed down enough and she slept the rest of the night.

Landero listened to her story, then with a quickened pulse took the jar out of the box and opened it. Lo and behold! The metal fetish had completely disintegrated and turned to grey powder! From that moment on, Manuel Sena was liberated from the demons.[4]

One of the products of this spontaneous combustion movement has been a remarkably well organized and effective program of grassroots social service, organized by Victor Landero's younger brother, Gregorio. It is not some imported program, but springs from local initiative. Through their organization called *Acción Unida* new industries have been established, farmers have begun to produce for the commercial market as well as just for their families, epidemics have been stayed, savings and loan agencies have been set up, people are learning to read and write, and new prosperity has begun to cover the area, benefiting both believers and unbelievers.[5]

But the church is growing. In 1960 this group of Christians met in ten organized churches and fifteen newer congregations. Today they number forty-seven churches and eighty-six congregations. These are all actively planting daughter churches, and 105 new spiritual children are in one stage or another of gestation. The larger churches run to 300 members. The annual rate of growth is currently a healthy fifteen percent to twenty percent. To keep pace with such rapid growth, leadership patterns have changed also. In 1960 the churches had twelve pastors, all trained in traditional seminaries. Today only two seminary-trained pastors remain. The work is carried on by sixty other full-supported workers plus sixty-four additional workers who earn their own living.

One of the interesting things about these churches is that they dislike the word, "Pentecostal." They strongly object if anyone refers to them as Pentecostal churches. They prefer "renewal." They are affiliated with the Association of Evangelical Churches of the Caribbean, a non-Pentecostal denomination which grew out of the Latin America Mission. As non-Pentecostal churches, however, they act like Pentecostals, they look a great deal like Pentecostals, and more important they also *grow* like Pentecostals. If they will pardon my saying it, here, by spontaneous combustion, the Pentecostal movement has entered non-Pentecostal churches. Call it what you may, the brothers and sisters there are delighted at the way the Holy Spirit is using them in their area.

If you asked the leader of almost any non-Pentecostal church (or of some decadent Pentecostal churches as well), "Wouldn't you like the Lord to use you like he is using Victor Landero and the others in Colombia?", the response would almost invariably be, "Yes." Most Christians covet that kind of joy, enthusiasm, and effectiveness in reaching their community. But despite this honest desire, many evangelicals still oppose "Pentecostalizing tendencies." This is not new. It happened back in the days of Hoover in Chile. After the Methodist Pentecostal Church split off from them, the Methodists who remained reacted so strongly that they even stopped saying "Amen" in their services. They discontinued personal evangelism, open air preaching, and prayer meetings just so they wouldn't look very much like Pentecostals.[6] The Methodist missionaries also failed to see that the new Pentecostal movement was something authentically Chilean, not merely an extension of Hoover's views. Deep down, the Chileans in the Methodist Pentecostal Church blamed the missionaries for the stifling of the Holy Spirit's activity in their former church.[7]

In his message to the Congress on Evangelization, Rubén Lores inferred as much. "We see all over," he said, "a growing sense of impatience with the foreign missions and with the ecclesiastical structures they have created." He pled for new freedom in all of the churches for the Holy Spirit to act as He will. "Are we by some stretch of the imagination agencies of a commercial enterprise directed from New York or Geneva?" he asked the delegates. "Let us allow the Holy Spirit to be truly Lord," he concluded, "because the Lord is that Spirit; and where the Spirit of the Lord is, there is liberty."[8]

It is bad enough for non-Pentecostals to ignore

what the Spirit is doing through Pentecostal brethren. This becomes even worse, however, when some actively and officially oppose such movings of God. This opposition most frequently is couched in doctrinal terminology. I have a copy of an official denominational policy statement before me which illustrates how this can go to an extreme. I will not reveal the source, except to point out that the denomination was founded by an evangelical mission and that foreign missionary influence in the national church is still considerable, although not total. In this particular country, the renewal movement in non-Pentecostal churches has been strong, provoking such a policy formulation. Here is a portion of the document, literally translated from the Spanish:

> Recently some non-Pentecostal groups have arisen which attempt to bring into their meetings such Pentecostal customs and practices as clapping while singing, worldly music, and the excessive use of sacred expressions like hallelujahs and amens with no thought as to the meaning of such expressions. . . . We believe that the current fad of speaking in tongues is not regulated by Holy Scripture. . . . We advise those brethren in our own churches who have Pentecostal tendencies to seek their fellowship somewhere else rather than try to change our long-standing tradition. . . .

We can only feel sorry for a church which can find no room in its fellowship for brethren such as we have been describing in this book. This attitude is completely the opposite of the approach that David Howard, Director of the Colombian field of the Latin America Mission, took when he dealt with the Pentecostal manifestations there.

Howard, who had no Pentecostal inclinations himself, said that when he found charismatic manifestations among the brethren in the Colombian forest, he felt like Peter did when God lowered the great sheet full of unclean animals in Acts 10. God spoke to him as he did to Peter. He told Peter to accept the Gentiles. He told David Howard to accept the charismatic brethren. Howard testifies that "slowly, God removed our skepticism, confirming the gifts of the Spirit by showing the fruit of the Spirit in the lives of the believers who received these gifts. . . . They showed more love, joy, peace, and other Christian attributes than many Christians who have known the Lord for years." [9] Howard and his colleagues exercised Christian patience and tolerance in what was for them an unusual and difficult situation. They have never regretted it, for the Spirit of God has continued to work in many extraordinary ways, and most of all, the Lord is adding *daily* to the church such as should be saved.

As I have attempted to study the broader scope of the charismatic movement in Latin America, I have come across the most precise data on Colombia, Brazil, Chile, Argentina, and Costa Rica. The First Latin American Renewal Congress, held in Buenos Aires in 1972, brought together eighty top leaders of what they prefer to call the "renewal movement" from the countries I have mentioned, plus Paraguay and Ecuador.[10] The Second Congress was held in Porto Alegre, Brazil, in January, 1973. The number of delegates soared from eighty to 2,000, and Uruguay joined the nations represented.[11] One of the reasons why these leaders prefer "renewal" to "Pentecostal" as an adjective describing their movement is that some Pentecostal leaders themselves confess that they are as much in need of renewal as the more traditional churches.

The renewal movement in Latin America is so new that not much is yet known about it. Someone needs to go deeper to find the answers to some tantilizing questions. For example, is it just conincidence that the renewal movement seems to be taking root faster in the most European of the Latin American republics (such as Argentina, Brazil, Chile, Uruguay, and Costa Rica), while it has not seemed to catch on equally well in the most Indian republics (such as Mexico, Guatemala, Peru, and Bolivia)? I do not have the answer to this question, but I hope someone finds it.

In Brazil, one recent study[12] estimates the number of Protestants in the charismatic movement at 60,000. The consistent pattern there is a split from the traditional denomination which would not allow the charismatic gifts. The Wesleyan Church, for example, broke off from the Methodist Church in 1967. They now number 10,000, at least half of them having been newly converted from the world. The Baptists, Presbyterians, and Congregationalists all have suffered similar splits, with their charismatic membership forming separate churches. William Cook, a vigorous researcher of the movement, says that in Brazil "the movement has been increasingly plagued by disunity and rivalry among the leadership. Churches which at first grew rapidly are beginning to stagnate." [13]

In Chile, the Methodists apparently have learned their lesson. Certain Pentecostal manifestations have broken out in Methodist churches around the city of Tomé. Their worship services are almost like Pentecostal meetings. Whether they speak in tongues, I do not know. They actively witness for Christ and seek to lead others to God and to the church. Little wonder that these churches are growing faster than their sister Methodist churches in other parts of Chile, where more traditional patterns are followed. Some of the top Methodist leaders are outspoken in their admiration of the Tomé brethren, although others are more skeptical. But they have not as yet had to leave the Methodist church in order to allow the Spirit to work freely in their midst.[14]

In Colombia, the renewal movement led by Victor Landero has also spilled over into the Presbyterian churches. Some new Presbyterian churches have sprung up which do not resemble traditional Presbyterian churches very closely at all. Guitars, hand-clapping, faith healing, tongues, unpaid lay workers, and other characteristics set them apart from the others. Has this helped church growth? Dramatically! The movement began only three years ago. Already the number of Presbyterian community has risen from 1,000 to over 2,000 in that short time. Presbyterian churches in other parts of Colombia have become interested now, and perhaps the movement will spread even further afield. No mention of the necessity for a church split has been made as yet.[15]

Argentina has been the setting of one of the most publicized renewal movements in recent years.[16] Roots of this go back as far as 1963 or 1964 when Keith Bentson, an American missionary, began holding deeper life conferences in the traditional churches. His ministry was widely accepted in the Plymouth Brethren, Baptist, Mennonite, and other churches of the country. Bentson was not Pentecostal, but he began to encourage the brethren in those rather static churches to praise the Lord. He stressed praise, audible and visible praise, time and again. Some churches developed a new sense of spontaneous praise, and this in itself became a kind of renewal without charismatic manifestations. In the Buneos Aires area, a praise meeting held on Monday nights in the home of a wealthy Plymouth Brethren business executive, Alberto Darling, gained some fame, and most of the top Plymouth Brethren leaders attended from time to time.

In one of the meetings, the wife of one of the better known Plymouth Brethren evangelists spontaneously began to speak in tongues. The others, with hearts open to the Spirit's leading, accepted this as from God. But none of them knew much about charismatic gifts. They, following Darby, believed that the "sign gifts" ceased with the apostolic church. They could not deny what they had seen, however. So they called in Juan Carlos Ortíz, the dynamic pastor of a prominent Assemblies of God Church to help them interpret what was happening. Ortíz was fascinated by what he saw and he even said that at times, faced by such an evident manifestation of the Holy Spirit, he himself felt like an unbeliever needing to be rebaptized. Ortíz wisely did not emphasize charismatic gifts as much as he did the Lordship of Christ. But charismatic manifestations continued to become more and more common.

Something contagious was taking place. When

the Monday night group reached 120, they rented a hall which would hold more people, but they soon outgrew that as well. From there they moved to a local movie theater, *Cine Moreno*, and attendance rose to one thousand or more. Almost every evangelical leader in Argentina soon had attended at least one Monday night renewal meeting. Some were attracted to the movement but others reacted strongly against the hand-clapping, the gestures, the marching, and praying with uplifted hands.

The top Plymouth Brethren hierarchy divided on the issue. Some thought this should be taken to the churches, some condemned it as unspiritual and unscriptural. Because of their congregational structure, it could not be prohibited for all Plymouth Brethren churches. Each "assembly" had to make its own decision. Some of them became "renewed," and their meetings took on a definite Pentecostal style. By about 1970 it was estimated that 5,000 of the total 25,000 membership were participating in the renewal movement.

This same pattern carried over into the Baptist and Mennonite churches. No denominational splits have taken place, but some of the Baptist and Mennonite churches are commonly known as belonging to the so-called *"movimiento."* Even some of the traditional Pentecostal churches are more associated with the *movimiento* than others. One of the most deeply involved Pentecostal churches is the Hidalgo Church which Juan Carlos Ortíz himself pastors. Ortíz is considered by many as the "great organizer, the synthesizer of the reflection and practice of the group and the consumate communicator." [17]

Curiously, the *movimiento* in Argentina has not yet produced any dramatic increase in church growth as similar movements have in other countries. This is not because it misunderstands the mission of the church. The participants are all evangelistically minded. They seek to win others to Christ. Most of the leaders expect the breakthrough to be right around the corner, and they are ready for large church growth. But when I asked Keith Bentson recently why in five years few strides have been made in effective evangelism, he replied that no one really suspected just how sick the churches were before the Spirit began His work. The healing process took longer than anticipated, but Bentson expects good church growth soon.

Perhaps one reason why I am convinced that non-Pentecostal churches can learn much from the Pentecostals in Latin America is that our own church did. We belonged to one of the largest churches in the city of Cochabamba, Bolivia, called the Calle Bolivar Church. It was situated only one-half block from the central plaza in the middle of the city. It had an excellent location, but it had become very routine and nominal. The pastor was deeply concerned. He wanted to win people to Christ and plant new churches. But the inertia was almost overwhelming. The denomination, the U.C.E., had four churches in Cochabamba in 1964, and in 1969 there were still four. The city was growing, but the church wasn't. Members seemed to attend church from force of habit. Wide yawns, mentioned previously, were commonplace. Few had much desire to bring their non-Christian friends to church, because it just wasn't any fun.

Decisions for Christ were rare, and baptisms took place perhaps once or twice a year.

Then a Pentecostal pastor from Chile passed through town. The pastor of our church met him and learned of some of the things the Spirit of God was doing in Chile. He became so enthusiastic that he invited the Chilean to take his Sunday morning pulpit. Sunday morning sermons there were ordinarily twenty minutes long, but the Chilean held the congregation spellbound for a full hour. Among other things, he said, "I'll bet you people have been praying that the Lord would bring unbelievers into your church to be saved." He paused. Scores nodded their heads (in Chile they would have shouted!). Then he let a bomb fall. He frowned, pointed his finger and said, "But that prayer of yours is a sin! You have no right to ask the Lord to do something when He already has commanded you otherwise. You have been disobedient! You know very well that the Lord has commanded you to 'go and preach the Gospel to all creatures,' then you turn around and pray that He will bring them in without your going. God will not bless you unless you *go out* and take the Gospel to the people where they are!"

That was just what the church needed. The very next Sunday the church began going out, and up until we left Bolivia six months later it had continued. On the average Sunday night, thirty to forty believers would gather at the church door an hour before the service. Some would bring accordions, some guitars, some drums, and other instruments. Two or three would come with open pickup trucks. The pastor would form groups and send them out into the streets.

The open air meetings drew good crowds around the market places. When they were over, the leaders would invite the onlookers to climb into the trucks and come to church with them. Full truckloads of people would pull up to the church doors, and then the musicians would all congregate on the street in front of the church for the final meeting. Traffic would slow to a crawl. Invariably passers-by would come into the church. Then the musicians would all go up front and form an orchestra of sorts for the meeting. With a full church and lively music, it became fun to go to church once more.

As a result people began coming to Christ. From the time we began going out to the people and "Pentecostalizing" our services slightly, until the time we left Bolivia, not a Sunday night went by without from one to twenty-seven decisions for Christ. Baptisms were being held once a month instead of once a year. New congregations were being formed in several other places in the city. Although no charismatic manifestations were evident in this non-Pentecostal church, it did learn much from its Pentecostal brethren about how churches grow.

Even as this book goes to press an exciting development is taking place in Bolivia on a nation-wide basis. Julio César Ruibal, twenty, a Bolivian studying in Pasadena, California, was converted there under Kathryn Kuhlman in late 1971, and soon afterward discovered that he had the gift of healing. He returned to Bolivia to preach salvation and healing in January, 1973, and like the Apostle Paul, "turned the world upside down." It is too early as this is being written to evaluate the results of this widespread spiritual awakening in Bolivia in terms of church growth. But suffice it to say that Ruibal's ministry, decidedly a Pentecostal type, was accepted with unusual enthusiasm by evangelical leaders across the board, both Pentecostal and non-Pentecostal. It is a sign of the times!

The Templo Bíblico of San José, Costa Rica, was another church located in the middle of a capital city, but it had become dull and stagnant. I visited it once in 1963 and again ten years later in 1972. In 1962 I saw a healthy, growing church, but nothing spectacular. In 1972, however, I could hardly believe my eyes. When I went to Sunday morning service I had a difficult time finding a seat. Standing room only had become the norm. When the service started and people prayed with their hands lifted up, I had an inkling of what might have happened. Later I found out for sure.[18]

The church had taken a spiritual nosedive in the period 1967-1970. By 1970 attendance had dropped from 600 to 200 on Sunday morning and from 400 to about forty on Sunday night. Pessimism and depression had gripped the leaders. Personal problems plagued the choir, the Sunday School teachers, and even the board of elders. In desperation the trustees even grappled with the consideration of selling the property. They were ready to abandon the church and each go his own way. They prayed weakly that God would do something, and they themselves did as much as they could. They invited Alberto Mottesti, one of the Baptist pastors deeply involved in the renewal movement in Argentina, to minister to them. They also invited Juan Carlos Ortíz himself. Each of these men

of God contributed to the coming renewal movement, but the dramatic breakthrough had not yet
occurred.

Then the Lord sent someone they had not invited. He was Father Francis McNutt from Notre
Dame, an American priest who had become associated with the Catholic charismatic movement
in the United States. Few people at the Templo
Bíblico had ever even heard of him until the
news began to spread that he had come to Costa
Rica to preach renewal to the Catholics there.
Some evangelical leaders of the renewal movement, among them Rubén Lores, however, had
been informed of the development of these plans
from the beginning.[19]

The pastor and some of the elders of the Templo
Bíblico went to hear him in a private home,
by special invitation. It was a small meeting, with
only a few present. McNutt and a psychiatrist,
Mrs. Barbara Schalmann, gave their testimonies
of renewal. Afterwards all was quiet for a time.
An invitation to pray for the fulness of the Spirit
was given. Someone started crying and then began
laughing uncontrollably. Several others had a similar experience. The atmosphere was electric, and
the presence of the Holy Spirit was evident. Im-
pressed, the Protestants invited McNutt to speak
at the Templo Bíblico that next Sunday night.

They advertised the meeting on the radio. The
very novelty of having a Catholic Priest in a Protestant service for the first time was enough to
arouse curiosity and an overflow crowd packed
into the large building. Again, the priest and Sister
Schalmann repeated their simple testimonies. Then
things began to happen that had never before hap-

pened in the Templo Bíblico. The structured service was over, but spontaneously people began moving up front to pray, and McNutt laid his hands on some as he felt led. Some were singing, some were laughing, some began speaking in tongues, and some even singing in tongues.

Needless to say, the Templo Bíblico has never been the same. Juan Carlos Ortíz returned and provided a significant impulse to the budding movement. At least a dozen come to Christ every Sunday, sometimes many more. Remarkable conversions are the order of the day. The church is full Sunday morning and Sunday night. The attitude of the believers has changed. They invite their friends because now it is fun to go to church. Baptisms are frequent, with between twenty-five and 125 at each baptism. Sometimes the elders take turns baptizing, there are so many candidates. And new churches are starting in other parts of the city.

Now, the Templo Bíblico does not consider itself a Pentecostal church at all. It is a Bible Church in the evangelical tradition. It has not split off from any other group, nor does it plan to. The Association of Bible Churches it belongs to, although a non-Pentecostal denomination, is not bringing charges of one sort or another against the Templo Bíblico. Just the opposite. The experience of revival has begun to spread through sister churches in Costa Rica. In 1972 the Association invited Gregorio Landero of Colombia as the speaker for their general assembly meetings, with great blessing and joy for all.

An important question raised by many sincere Latin American leaders is this: can our Pentecostal brethren really teach us non-Pentecostals something? But even more basic is this question: is the Spirit of God saying something to us non-Pentecostals as we take an objective look at our Pentecostal brethren in Latin America?

Pentecostals are growing so rapidly that we ought to be deeply concerned with our own slow growth. Are we really that concerned? Are we concerned enough to go out in the forest like Victor Landero to fast and pray with tears? If not, we may be found guilty of quenching the Spirit. Unwittingly, we ourselves may be obstacles to the evangelization of the fourth world in Latin America rather than clear channels of salvation. But the prayer of concern will only be answered if we have open minds and open hearts. The Spirit needs freedom to work. And when He works, He in turn brings freedom.

As I conclude this book, I feel remarkably identified with my namesake, the Apostle Peter, when he returned to his brethren in Jerusalem after visiting Cornelius' house. They were horrified that he, a Jew, had eaten unclean food in the house of a Gentile. Peter had to explain to them that it wasn't some scheme of his own, but that it was something God had required him to do. Peter wasn't about to become a Gentile, and as far as we know he never ate unclean food again. Nor was anyone requiring other Jewish Christians to stop being Jews. What God was trying to teach those Jewish Christians, and what he may be trying to teach us non-Pentecostals, is that they should be open to the working of the Holy Spirit whether or not it conforms to our own traditions and patterns.

Peter, a Jew, told his Jewish brethren what God was doing over there with the Gentiles. I, a non-Pentecostal, have told my non-Pentecostal brethren what God is doing over there with the Pentecostals. Can we not all agree with Peter's very simple statement, "Since it was God . . . who was I to argue?" (Acts 11:17, *Living Bible*)

The influence of the Pentecostal movement in Latin America will almost certainly increase in non-Pentecostal churches in the forseeable future. God will bless the churches which are prepared for this, and which are anxious for new power and effectiveness and growth. The appeal is not that they become Pentecostal churches. The appeal is that we all learn from each other, and that together, Pentecostals and non-Pentecostals, we be "endued with power from on high," and move out to win the multitudes of Latin America to Jesus Christ.

Notes

CHAPTER 1: THE PHENOMENAL GROWTH OF LATIN AMERICAN PENTECOSTALISM

1. See, e.g., Alan Walker, "Where Pentecostalism Is Mushrooming," *Christian Century* (Jan. 17, 1968), p. 81. Other estimates place membership below 200,000 as in Read, Monterroso, and Johnson, and others are in between. We have used the higher figure here, although the point would be made if we had used 200,000.

2. Information for the section on Hoover was taken from his book *Historia del Avivamiento Pentecostal en Chile.*

3. Arno Enns, *Man Milieu and Mission in Argentina* (Grand Rapids: Eerdmans), pp. 76-77.

4. Information for the section on Hicks came largely from a personal interview with him by the author at his Glendale, California, home, October 17, 1972, as

well as from his book, *Millions Found Christ* (Los Angeles: Manifest Deliverance and Worldwide Evangelism, Inc., 1956).

5. Hicks, p. 9.

6. Arno Enns, p. 206.

7. William Read, Victor Monterroso, and Harmon Johnson, *Latin American Church Growth* (Grand Rapids: Eerdmans, 1969), p. 381.

8. Data on the Brazil section has been taken from William Read, *New Patterns of Church Growth in Brazil*, from Read, Monterroso, and Johnson, as well as from a personal interview with Read, October 18, 1972.

9. John Thomas Nichol, *Pentecostalism*, pp. 132-133.

10. Emílio Conde, *Historia das Assembléias de Deus no Brasil* (Río de Janeiro, Assembléias de Deus, 1960), pp. 25-26.

CHAPTER 2: ENDUED WITH POWER
FROM ON HIGH

1. Willis C. Hoover, *Historia del Avivamiento Pentecostal en Chile* (Valparíso: Imprenta Excelsior, 1948), p. 31.

2. William Read, Victor Monterroso, and Harmon Johnson, *Latin American Church Growth* (Grand Rapids: Eerdmans, 1969), p. 37.

3. Alan Walker, "Where Pentecostalism Is Mushrooming," *Christian Century* (January 17, 1968), p. 81.

4. Luther P. Gerlach and Virginia H. Hine, "Five Factors Crucial to the Growth and Spread of a Modern Religious Movement," *Journal for the Scientific Study of Religion* (Spring, 1968), p. 32.

5. Read, Monterroso, and Johnson, pp. 318-319.

CHAPTER 3: TAKING THE GOSPEL
TO THE PEOPLE

1. For more information see Juan Carlos Ortíz and

Keith Bentson, ...y será predicado este evangelio (Buenos Aires: Editorial Logos, 1969).

2. Information on the Foursquare in Guayaquíl, Ecuador, was taken from Wayne Weld, *An Ecuadorian Impasse* (Chicago: Evangelical Covenant Church of America, 1968), and from a personal interview by the author of Roberto Aguirre, June 8, 1972. Aguirre was the Foursquare missionary in charge of the crusade. He claims over 4,000 baptized members in 1966, while Weld places 1966 membership at 1,868, and 1968 membership at 3,000.

CHAPTER 4: MOTHERS AND DAUGHTERS— CHURCH REPRODUCTION

1. The sources of information on the Foursquare Church in Ecuador are the same as indicated in note 2 for chapter three.

2. Donald C. Palmer, *The Growth of the Pentecostal Churches in Colombia* (Deerfield: Trinity Evangelical Divinity School, 1972), pp. 23-25.

3. *Ibid.*, p. 21.

4. Information on Brazil for Christ is taken from William Read, *New Patterns of Church Growth in Brazil*, pp. 144-158, and from Edward F. Murphy, *Brazil para Cristo* (Pasadena: Fuller Theological Seminary, unpublished research, 1972).

5. Murphy, pp. 37-41.

6. Read, Monterroso, and Johnson, *Latin American Church Growth* (Grand Rapids: Eerdmans, 1969), pp. 67-68.

7. *Ibid.*, p. 68.

8. J. B. A. Kessler, *A Study of the Older Protestant Missions and Churches in Peru and Chile* (Goes: Oosterbaan & le Cointre, 1967), p. 318.

9. Ignacio Vergara, *El Protestantismo en Chile* (Santiago: Editorial del Pacifico, 1962), p. 163.

10. Norbert E. Johnson, *The History, Dynamic and Problems of the Pentecostal Church in Chile* (Rich-

mond: Union Theological Seminary, unpublished Th.M. thesis, 1970), p. 52.

11. Kessler, p. 317.

CHAPTER 5: SOWING THE SEED ON FERTILE SOIL

1. Emilio Willems, *Followers of the New Faith* (Nashville: Vanderbilt University Press, 1967).

2. Christian Lalive, *Haven of the Masses* (London: Lutterworth Press, 1969).

3. Willems, p. 248.

4. Lalive, p. 224.

5. Donald McGavran, *Understanding Church Growth* (Grand Rapids: Eerdmans, 1970), pp. 260-277.

6. Lalive, pp. 215-216.

7. Alan Walker, "Where Pentecostalism is Mushrooming," *Christian Century* (Jan. 17, 1968), p. 82.

8. William Read, Victor Monterroso, and Harmon Johnson, *Latin American Church Growth* (Grand Rapids: Eerdmans, 1969), p. 356.

9. Norbert Johnson, *The History, Dynamic and Problems of the Pentecostal Church in Chile* (Richmond: Union Theological Seminary, unpublished Th.M. thesis, 1970), p. 56.

CHAPTER 6: BODY LIFE BUILDS HEALTHY CHURCHES

1. Ray Stedman, *Body Life* (Glendale: Regal Books, 1972).

2. Donald Palmer, *The Growth of Pentecostal Churches in Colombia* (Deerfield: Trinity Evangelical Divinity School, unpublished M.A. thesis, 1972), p. 108.

3. Walter Hollenweger, *The Pentecostals* (Minneapolis: Augsburg Press, 1972), pp. 85, 88.

4. Donald McGavran, *Understanding Church Growth* (Grand Rapids: Eerdmans, 1970), p. 15.

5. Palmer, p. 130.

6. Read, Monterroso, and Johnson, *Latin American Church Growth* (Grand Rapids: Eerdmans, 1969), p. 57.

7. Melvin Hodges, *Growing Young Churches* (Chicago: Moody Press, 1970), p. 47.

8. The most complete statements of the "syndrome of church development" are found in C. Peter Wagner, *Frontiers in Missionary Strategy* (Chicago: Moody Press, 1971), pp. 169-171, and C. Peter Wagner, ed., *Church/Mission Tensions Today* (Chicago: Moody Press, 1972), pp. 215-232.

9. Assemblies of God, *Missionary Manual* (Springfield: Foreign Missions Department) n.p.

CHAPTER 7: SEMINARIES IN THE STREETS

1. David Brackenridge, "Pentecostal Progress in Chile," *World Dominion* (Sept.-Oct., 1951), p. 296.

2. Christian Lalive, *Haven of the Masses* (London: Lutterworth Press, 1969), p. 70.

3. Donald McGavran, *Understanding Church Growth* (Grand Rapids: Eerdmans, 1970), pp. 260-277.

4. Lalive, p. 72.

5. This has also been described in *An Extension Seminary Primer* by Ralph R. Covell and C. Peter Wagner (South Pasadena: William Carey Library, 1971), pp. 66-67.

6. Melvin Hodges, *Growing Young Churches* (Chicago: Moody Press, 1970), p. 62.

7. The best sources to date are Covell and Wagner and Ralph Winter, ed., *Theological Education by Extension* (South Pasadena: William Carey Library, 1969).

CHAPTER 8: IT'S FUN TO GO TO CHURCH

1. Emilio Castro, "Pentecostalism and Ecumenism in Latin America," *Christian Century*, (September 27, 1972), p. 955.

2. J. B. A. Kessler, *A Study of the Older Protestant*

Missions and Churches in Peru and Chile (Goes: Oosterbaan & le Cointre, 1967), p. 323.

3. Howard A. Snyder, "The People of God—Implications for Church Structure," *Christianity Today*, (Oct. 27, 1972), p. 9.

4. Eugene Nida, "The Indigenous Churches in Latin America" (Buck Hill Falls: C.C.L.A., 1960), p. 10.

5. Donald Palmer, *The Growth of the Pentecostal Churches in Colombia* (Deerfield: Trinity Evangelical Divinity School, unpublished M.A. thesis, 1972), p. 124.

6. *Ibid.*, p. 60.

7. Nida, p. 8.

CHAPTER 9: PRAYING FOR THE SICK

1. Manuel Gaxiola, *La Serpiente y la Paloma* (South Pasadena: William Carey Library, 1970), p. 7.

2. This data was taken from notes on a personal interview by the author with Roberto Aguirre, June 8, 1972.

3. Christian Lalive, *Haven of the Masses* (London: Lutterworth Press, 1969), pp. 197, 204.

4. Read, Monterroso, and Johnson, *Latin American Church Growth* (Grand Rapids: Eerdmans, 1969), p. 323.

5. This story was told to Lalive, pp. 205-205.

6. Donald Palmer, *The Growth of the Pentecostal Churches in Colombia* (Deerfield: Trinity, Evangelical Divinity School, unpublished M.A. thesis, 1972), p. 116.

7. Gaxiola, p. 10.

8. Palmer, p. 63.

9. Tommy Hicks, *Millions Found Christ* (Los Angeles: Manifest Deliverance and Worldwide Evangelism, Inc., 1956), pp. 21-23.

10. Edward Murphy, *Brazil Para Cristo* (Pasadena: Fuller Theological Seminary, 1972), pp. 16-20.

11. Harmon Johnson, *Authority Over the Spirits: Brazilian Spiritism and Evangelical Church Growth*

(Pasadena: Fuller Theological Seminary, 1969), unpublished M.A. thesis.
    12. *Ibid.*, p. 91.
    13. *Ibid.*, pp. 102-103.
    14. *Ibid.*, p. 110.

CHAPTER 10: ARE PENTECOSTALS ON A "SOCIAL STRIKE"?

    1. Christian Lalive, *Haven of the Masses* (London: Lutterworth Press, 1969), p. 145.
    2. *Ibid.*, p. 144.
    3. See Emilio Willems, *Followers of the New Faith* (Nashville: Vanderbilt University Press, 1967).
    4. William Winston Elliott, *Sociocultural Change in a Pentecostal Group* (Knoxville: University of Tennessee, D.Ed. dissertation, 1971), p. 212.
    5. Lalive, p. 140.
    6. Dean M. Kelley, *Why Conservative Churches Are Growing* (New York: Harper and Row, 1972), p. 95.
    7. *Ibid.*, p. 89.
    8. *Ibid.*, p. 84.
    9. *Ibid.*, p. 146
    10. *Ibid.*, p. 147.
    11. *Ibid.*, p. 37.
    12. *Ibid.*, p. 45.
    13. Donald Palmer, *The Growth of Pentecostal Churches in Colombia* (Deerfield: Trinity Evangelical Divinity School, unpublished M.A. thesis, 1972), p. 147.
    14. *Ibid.*, p. 150.
    15. *Ibid.*, p. 73.
    16. Justo L. González, *The Development of Christianity in the Latin Caribbean* (Grand Rapids: Eerdmans, 1969), p. 119.
    17. Melvin L. Hodges, "A Pentecostal's View of Mission Strategy," *International Review of Missions,* (July, 1968), p. 309.
    18. Palmer, p. 117.
    19. J. B. A. Kessler, *A Study of the Older Protestant*

Missions and Churches in Peru and Chile (Goes: Oosterbaan & le Cointre, 1967), p. 292.

20. Willems, p. 148.

21. Walter J. Hollenweger, *The Pentecostals* (Minneapolis: Augsburg, 1972), p. 80.

CHAPTER 11: PENTECOSTALS
IN NON-PENTECOSTAL CHURCHES

1. Rubeń Lores, "Sobre Toda Carne," *Acción en Cristo para un Continente en Crisis* (Miami: Editorial Caribe, 1970), p. 11.

2. Information on the Colombian movement under Victor Landero was taken from David Howard, *Hammered as Gold* (New York: Harper & Row, 1969), and from a personal interview with Gregorio Landero, November 7, 1972.

3. Howard, pp. 122-124.

4. *Ibid.*, pp. 152-153.

5. See Kenyon, "Gregorio Landero: He Helps Colombia's Forgotten People."

6. J.B.A. Kessler, *A Study of the Older Protestant Missions*, p. 127.

7. *Ibid.*

8. Lores, *op. cit.*, p. 13.

9. Howard, *op. cit.*, p. 146.

10. Orlando Costas, "Dateline Buenos Aires," p. 22.

11. A. William Cook, Jr., "Church Renewal in Latin America," typescript of report of the Eighth Annual Conference of the Brazilian Charismatic Renewal Movement and the Second Latin American Renewal Congress, January 20-28, 1973. Porto Alegre, Brazil, p. 1. Cook is one of the most active current researchers of the Latin American renewal movement.

12. William R. Read, "A Charismatic Stream Flows in Brazil."

13. *Ibid.*

14. Read, Monterroso, and Johnson, *Latin American Church Growth*, p. 380.

15. Charles Bennett, "Notable Church Multiplication in Colombia," p. 86.

16. Information on the renewal movement in Argentina was taken from a personal interview with Peter Larson, November 21, 1972; from his paper, "El Movimiento de Renovación, Buenos Aires, Argentina;" and from my own personal knowledge of the movement.

17. A. William Cook, Jr. Personal letter to author, February 12, 1973.

18. Information on the renewal in San José, Costa Rica, was taken from notes on a message by Victor Monterroso in September, 1972; from information supplied by A. William Cook, Jr. and Rubén Lores; and from personal knowledge of the situation.

19. A. William Cook, Jr., typescript of research paper presented to the faculty of the Latin American Biblical Seminary, San José, Costa Rica, n.d., p. 16.

Bibliography

Assemblies of God, *Missionary Manual.* Springfield: Foreign Missions Department, unpublished typescript, 1972.

Bennett, Charles. "Notable Church Multiplication in Colombia," *Church Growth Bulletin* (September, 1970), pp. 85-87.

Brackenridge, David C. "Pentecostal Progress in Chile," *World Dominion* (September-October, 1951), pp. 295-298.

Castro, Emilio. "Pentecostalism and Ecumenism in Latin America," *Christian Century* (September 27, 1972), pp. 955-957.

Conde, Emílio. *História das Assembléias de Deus no Brasil.* Río de Janeiro: Assembléias de Deus, 1960.

Cook, A. William, Jr.

Costas, Orlando. "Dateline Buenos Aires," *World Vision* (May, 1972), p. 22.

Covell, Ralph R. and C. Peter Wagner. *An Extension Seminary Primer.* South Pasadena: William Carey Library, 1971.

Elliott, William Winston, *Sociocultural Change in a Pentecostal Group: A Case Study in Education and Culture of the Church of God in Sonova, Mexico.* Knoxville: University of Tennessee, D.Ed. dissertation, 1971.

Enns, Arno W. *Man, Milieu and Mission in Argentina.* Grand Rapids; Eerdmans, 1971.

Escobar, Samuel, ed., *Accion en Cristo para un Continente en Crisis.* Miami: Editorial Caribe, 1970.

Gaxiola, Manuel J. *La Serpiente y la Paloma.* South Pasadena: William Carey Library, 1970.

Gerlach, Luther P. and Hine, Virginia H., "Five Factors Crucial to the Growth and Spread of a Modern Religious Movement," *Journal for the Scientific Study of Religion* (Spring, 1968, Volume VII, Number 1), pp. 23-40.

González, Justo L. *The Development of Christianity in the Latin Caribbean.* Grand Rapids: Eerdmans, 1969.

Hicks, Tommy. *Millions Found Christ.* Los Angeles: Manifest Deliverance and Worldwide Evangelism, Inc., 1956.

Hodges, Melvin L. "A Pentecostal's View of Mission Strategy," *International Review of Missions* (July, 1968), pp. 304-310.

_____. *Growing Young Churches.* Chicago: Moody Press, 1970.

Hollenweger, Walter J. *The Pentecostals, The Charismatic Movement in the Churches.* Minneapolis: Augsburg, 1972.

Hoover, W. C. *Historia del Avivamiento Pentecostal en Chile.* Valparíso: Imprenta Excelsior, 1948.

Howard, David M. *Hammered As Gold.* New York: Harper and Row, 1969.

Johnson, Harmon A. *Authority over the Spirits: Brazilian Spiritism and Evangelical Church Growth.* Pasadena: Fuller Theological Seminary School of World Mission, unpublished M.A. thesis, 1969.

Johnson, Norbert E. *The History, Dynamic and Problems of the Pentecostal Church in Chile.* Richmond: Union Theological Seminary, unpublished Th.M. thesis, 1970.

Kelley, Dean M. *Why Conservative Churches Are Growing.* New York: Harper and Row, 1972.

Kenyon, John. "Gregorio Landero: He Helps Colombia's Forgotten People," *Latin America Evangelist* (November-December, 1972).

Kessler, J. B. A. *A Study of the Older Protestant Missions and Churches in Peru and Chile.* Goes: Oosterbaan & le Cointre, 1967.

Lalive d'Epinay, Christian. *Haven of the Masses.* London: Lutterworth Press, 1969.

Larson, Peter. "El Movimiento de Renovación, Buenos Aires, Argentina." Pasadena: Fuller Theological Seminary School of World Mission, unpublished research project, 1972.

Lores, Rubén. "Sobre Toda Carne," *Acción en Cristo para un Continente en Crisis*, Samuel Escobar, ed. Miami: Editorial Caribe, 1970, pp. 11-13.

McGavran, Donald. *Understanding Church Growth.* Grand Rapids: Eerdmans, 1970.

Murphy, Edward F. *Brasil para Cristo.* Pasadena: Fuller Theological Seminary School of World Mission, unpublished research study project, 1972.

Nida, Eugene A. "The Indigenous Churches in Latin America." Buck Hill Falls, C.C.L.A., 1960.

Ortíz, Juan Carlos and Keith Bentson. *... y será predicado este evangelio..* Buenos Aires: Editorial Logos, 1969.

Palmer, Donald C. *The Growth of the Pentecostal Churches in Colombia.* Deerfield: Trinity Evangelical Divinity School, unpublished M.A. thesis, 1972.

Read, William R. "A Charismatic Stream Flows in Brazil," unpublished private document, 1972.

Read, William R., Victor M. Monterroso, and Harmon A. Johnson. *Latin American Church Growth.* Grand Rapids: Eerdmans, 1969.

Snyder, Howard A. "The People of God—Implications for Church Structure," *Christianity Today* (October 27, 1972), pp. 6-10.

Stedman, Ray C. *Body Life.* Glendale: Regal Books, 1972.

Vergara, Ignacio. *El protestantismo en Chile.* Santiago: Editorial del Pacífico, 1962.

Wagner, C. Peter. *Frontiers in Missionary Strategy.* Chicago: Moody Press, 1971.

_____, ed. *Church/Mission Tensions Today.* Chicago: Moody Press, 1972.

Walker, Alan. "Where Pentecostalism is Mushrooming," *Christian Century* (January 17, 1968), pp. 81-82.

Weld, Wayne C. *An Ecuadorian Impasse.* Chicago: Evangelical Covenant Church of America, 1968.

Willems, Emilio, *Followers of the New Faith.* Nashville: Vanderbilt University Press, 1967.

Winter, Ralph D., ed. *Theological Education by Extension.* South Pasadena: William Carey Library, 1969.

Index

B

Baptism, 48-49

Baptism in the Spirit, 34, 36

Baptismal regeneration, 48

Baptists, 24-25, 70, 123, 142, 160, 162, 163, 167

Belém, 24

Bentson, Keith, 161, 164

Berg, Daniel, 24-25, 27

Bigness, 107

Black Muslims, 140

Body life, 77-88

Bogotá, 149

Bolivia, 37, 59-61, 122, 160, 164-166

Brackenridge, David, 91

"brain drain," 105

Brás, Brazil, 23, 81

Brazil, 22-25, 26, 81, 138, 140, 147, 150, 159, 160

Brazil for Christ Church, 57-59, 81, 108, 116-117, 132-133

Buenos Aires, 18, 20, 22-23, 48, 50, 108, 130, 159, 162

Bultmann, Rudolph, 86

C

California, 125

Calle Bolivar Church, 164-166

Canada, 18

"Canutos," 41

Castro, Emilio, 101

Catholic charismatic Movement, U.S.A., 168

Catholics, 48, 73, 84

Centrifugal, 44

Centripetal, 44

Cerullo, Morris, 128

Charismatic movement, 150

Chávez, Enrique, 62

Chile, 15-18, 22, 26, 37, 62, 69, 89-92, 102, 111, 131, 137, 140-141, 146, 150, 157, 159-160, 165

Chilean Pentecostals, 42, 69, 72, 11, 138

Christian Church of North America, 22

Church-centeredness, 44, 50, 51

Church multiplication, 56

Church planting, 87, 141

Church splits, 62

Cine Moreno, 163

Clapping, 116

Classes, 94

Clergy, 93

Clergy-laity gap, 111

Cochabamba, Bolivia, 46-47, 122, 164-166

Colombia, 26, 37-39, 56-57, 83, 110, 129, 143, 150-151, 159, 161

Graham, Billy, 50
Great Commission, 46, 48, 67, 83, 37
"Great White Father," 102
Growth by splitting, 62
Guatemala, 150, 160
Guayaquíl, Ecuador, 50-51, 53-56, 124-126

H

Hacienda system, 68
Haiti, 134
Healing, 121-136
Healing vs. miracles, 130
Hicks, Tommy, 19-22, 27, 128, 130-131
Hidalgo Church, 108, 163
Hodges, Melvin, 85, 144
Holy Spirit, 29-31, 33-35, 40, 53, 69, 79-81, 86, 96, 103-105, 148
Honduras, 26
Hoover, Willis C., 16-18, 20, 27, 30-31, 63, 69, 89, 102, 146, 157
Howard, David, 158
Hymnology, 116

I

India, 17
Indigenous church, 105
Industrialization, 68

Institutional missions, 86
Interchurch aid, 86
Interpretation, 154
Italians, 22-23

J

Jehovah's Witnesses, 38, 140
"Jesus Only," 37, 39, 143
Jews, 170-171
John, 121
Johnson, Harmon, 133-136
See also Read, Monterroso and Johnson
Johnson, Norbert, 74
Jotabeche Church, 41, 43-44, 77-78, 89-92, 108, 131
Jiménez, Raimundo, 121, 131

K

Kelley, Dean, 139-142, 144
Kessler, J. B. A., 62-63, 102
Kneeling to pray, 111
Kuhlman, Kathryn, 166

L

Lalive, Christian, 68-69, 72, 137, 140-141

Sunday School teachers, 96

Syndrome of church development, 87, 103, 105

T

Tallahassee, Florida, 19
Templo Bíblico, 167-169
Temuco, Chile, 20
Theological education by extension, 99
Theology of search, 32
Tomé, Chile, 161
Tongues, 34, 36, 69, 113, 121, 123, 154
Trinity, 38

U

U.C.E., 164
UNELAM, 101
United Pentecostals, 37-39, 56, 80, 129, 143
Urbanization, 68
Uruguay, 128, 159-160

V

Valparaíso, Chile, 15, 146
Vásguez, Javier, 77-78, 89-92
Vatican II, 73
Venezuela, 128
Vingren, Gunnar, 24-25, 27
Volunteer corps, 78

W

Walker, Alan, 72
Ward, Ted, 92
Watts, Isaac, 105
Wesley, Charles, 72
Wesleyan Church, 160
Westminster Cathedral, 109
Willems, Emilio, 68, 138
Winter, Ralph, 92
Witchcraft, 127, 154-155
Witness, 82
World Council of Churches, 92, 101, 137, 145
Worship, 111

Scripture References